Praise for *Make the SHIFT*

"Written from the perspective of experience, *Make the SHIFT* is both high level and granular; thought provoking and actionable. A weekend read that could change the outcome of your company.

"A holistic approach to achieving new initiatives, *Make the SHIFT* uncovers the human element that hinders or harnesses change. *Make the SHIFT* helps you master the interplay of the human element with the implementation of your business plan and guides you to reaching your goals.

"I engaged Beverly and her team at The Collaborative to help me 'Make the SHIFT' from a developed idea to a company launch. I encourage you to take advantage of the wisdom within *Make the SHIFT*."

— *Mary Ann Buchanan, CEO and Founder of RIA Match*

"*Make the SHIFT* is like having a portable success coach in your pocket. It's a practical how-to guide for goal setting and business development that will leave you feeling inspired and ready to take action."

— *Lisa Bosley, Director, AUM Partners, LLC*

"*SHIFT* is a brilliant book bridging interpersonal coaching processes with the more corporate approach of business consulting. Combining the best of both worlds, Bev's book provides a whole new approach to healing the rifts that often destroy the fabric of trust so needed in building exceptional organizations."

— *Stephen Garrett, MA*
Presenter, Trainer, Author and Not Your Everyday Life Coach

"The SHIFT Model is an effective process by which our student teams explore complex real-world challenges, develop solutions, and prepare implementation recommendations."

— *Laurie Levesque, Associate Dean, Sawyer Business School, Suffolk University*

"This book is 'must reading' if you are interested in making a shift in your life. In this book, Beverly Flaxington demonstrates her practical understanding of the quantum connectedness that is our life system. She explains plainly and convincingly that every action we take has a 360-degree impact on all the system elements, and that high-quality decision making and effective life changes must take these system implications into consideration if we are to successfully cross the chasm from our current situation to our most desired situation. Ms. Flaxington demonstrates practical wisdom and functional steps in her new book, a rare treat honed in the crucible of her vast experiences."

— Dr. Ronald D. Cruickshank, author, inventor and mind coach

"Bev Flaxington has unique insights on the functioning of high performing teams, and *Make the SHIFT* provides any corporate team leader with the tools and perspectives they need to develop and execute strategies and plans that produce results."

—Scott C. Sacco, President and Founder Maquan Communications, LLC

"What makes people anxious about change is predicting an unknown future. SHIFT gives a concrete present."

—Janet Britcher, President, Transformation Management LLC

Make the Shift:

The Proven 5-Step Plan to Success for Corporate Teams

Beverly D. Flaxington

ATA Press

Published by ATA Press

ISBN 978-0-9837620-1-0

Library of Congress Control Number 2011913937

First printing: October, 2011

Table of Contents

This book is dedicated to a client I have long enjoyed working with, **Waldemar Kohl**.

Waldemar is the one who, over coffee one day, said, "You need to create a model that outlines what you do so well. It's different from other consultants and it works!" I went back to my desk that same day and defined the S.H.I.F.T. Model™.

Thank you, Waldemar — your words inspired me!

Foreword

Janet Powers, Chief Executive Diva
Diva Toolbox, LLC

Make the *SHIFT* should be on the desk of every business owner and executive. There are so many business owners just doing for the sake of doing, and the result is never really achieving; they are always still trying to get "there." Beverly describes easy and clever strategies for identifying, addressing, and solving what is stopping a business from getting to the next level. She explains how we may be working against our progress instead of for our progress simply by not seeing what's stopping us. My favorite line in the book is—"highlight your obstacles and categorize them." When you face the obstacles, you take away their power and you move forward...I know it because the day after I read the book I put these suggestions into action and saw it work firsthand in my business—you will, too!

Introduction

There are thousands of books on goal setting and change for businesses. Why do we need yet another book that examines these topics?

The answer is simple: Because this book is different. It stands apart from everything that's out there. Most books on goal setting and change management focus on technical information or complex theories developed by academics. This book concentrates on providing a no-nonsense, practical guide to help you understand fundamental precepts about what makes a business successful. It offers a new and innovative approach to goal setting and change management. It shows business owners and managers exactly what it takes to successfully shift a business in a new and (hopefully) more profitable direction.

This is not your standard goal-setting business book. If you've read a book or perhaps a magazine article on business goal setting and development, you've probably come across the standard approach to goal setting and business planning. What I call the standard ideas are basically those that feature in just about every one of those books on the typical business bookshelves.

Every standard approach tells you the importance of having goals that are, for instance, SMART—that is, specific, measurable, attainable, realistic, and time bound. They also tell you the importance of having a business plan. Sometimes, you're even told that a business plan should be developed in conjunction with a couple of other specific plans—marketing and strategic plans, for instance. These things also have merit. We'll talk about the importance of incorporating many of them within this process. But the "standard" approach fails to address some of the fundamental issues that get in the way of even the best-laid business plans.

In the last twenty-five years, I have taken on a variety of roles in business. I have been a corporate consultant, a senior level executive, a college professor teaching business courses, and a professional coach. In various capacities, I have worked with business owners and managers to bring about positive change in their professional and personal lives. I've observed many of the standard methods of goal setting and goal achievement in action. I've seen firsthand that often they simply don't work, and I've learned why. The closer you look at the many standard approaches, the clearer it is that they overlook key aspects of how we operate as human beings.

Even with SMART goals and detailed business plans, the process of sustaining the effort to change is often left to chance. And that is the problem.

Human beings are responsible for change, whether it is personal or business change. Every effort to create change is susceptible to the same problem. Change requires commitment—awareness, understanding, buy-in, and action.

Here is the bottom line, though. Whether you are an entry-level team member trying to improve your understanding of business operations or the CEO of a company looking for a way to shift your business into overdrive, the key ideas offered in this book can set you on the road to business success.

For the first time ever, you're getting access to a seminal process tailored specifically to the business community. This book looks at the resistance to success we all experience, and shows you a way to break free of it. The ideas I'm talking about here are also outlined in a step-by-step fashion so you can put them into practice right away. They are not esoteric theories or complicated concepts, but rather clear steps you can take to shift your business in a new direction.

As you read through the process, take the time to complete each step. Going through the process and applying it to your own experience is the key to success in your shift. Getting from here to there is never easy, but it's far from impossible—especially if you have a guide. You *can* move from here to there successfully, and in the next few pages I will show you just how to do it.

Book Structure

This book is divided into two sections. Part I discusses the specific steps of implementing the proven five-step process to enable your business to shift, and Part II discusses helpful tips and tools that have worked for literally thousands of business people I have shared them with over the years.

Part I is arranged as a step-by-step process with specific elements to focus on in sequential order. The S.H.I.F.T. Model™ 5-step process is intended to be used in order—the first step is labeled as "S," the next as "H," and so on. The process was also created as a change model. It works for anything you need to change—from the simple stuff like getting along with a colleague to things that are far more complicated, like re-engineering a team within a company. The only thing that changes is the manner in which you approach the steps. That will differ depending on your end goal. Don't skip any of the steps, though, because it will mean that your team won't end up developing a plan as thoroughly as is needed.

To help clarify what happens at each step, the book will follow a real person working through the process as well. Meet Todd Galant—he runs a successful firm, but is frustrated with his inability to keep a top-performing employee in a certain role. We used the S.H.I.F.T. Model™ on Todd's firm to find ideas he could implement going forward.

At the end of Part I, you will have everything in place to finally make the successful leap—a leap you may have tried unsuccessfully before—from where you are now to where you want to be.

Part II is structured in a looser format, with methods, tools, and tips that will make your transition more productive. Learning and internalizing them will make the shifting process easier and more effective.

It's possible to read either Part I or Part II of this book separately. Both parts are designed to work as stand-alone reference works. They complement each other, too, so the second strengthens the effect of the first. To get the most out of the book, you should read it in its entirety.

In any event, whatever your team decides to do, it's important to commit to do something. I've seen situations in which a business unit or a leader within an organization made even a minor shift—learned to do just one thing better and more effectively. They created a ripple effect that made many areas of their business better. I often liken the process to investing in a particular security within a portfolio of investments: Finding a strong performer may give the overall portfolio the percentage lift it needs to show strong performance in its entirety. This process is like that. You don't need to change everything, or have your organization become a perfectly oiled machine. But doing something differently that contributes to a positive change in just one area may give your entire organization a much-needed lift. At a minimum, every corporate team embarking on a change effort needs to follow the S.H.I.F.T. Model™. Used properly, it will ensure they have accurately captured where they are and that they created a clear plan for where they want to be.

NOTE:

Downloadable versions of all the worksheets included in this book may be found at **www.the-collaborative.com/shift-worksheets**

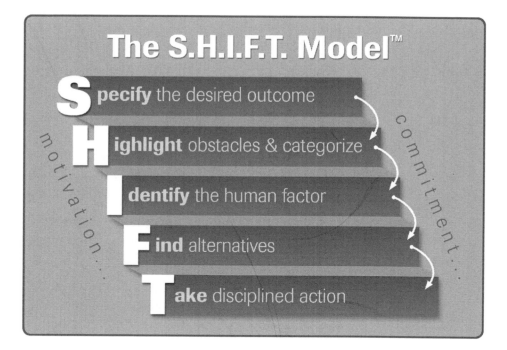

The S.H.I.F.T. Model™

Specify the desired outcome

Highlight obstacles & categorize

Identify the human factor

Find alternatives

Take disciplined action

motivation...

commitment...

PART I

The S.H.I.F.T. Model™

The S.H.I.F.T. Model™ is the result of decades of working with corporations. Over the years, I began to notice, when I worked with corporate clients on business building or change management, that I was taking the same steps to uncover real workable solutions as I did when working with individuals through coaching, hypnosis, training, or other behavioral change initiatives. The steps may seem almost self-evident once you understand them, but many of us simply can't afford to take the time to look up from the daily grind long enough to see the obvious.

I believe most efforts to bring about business change do not take the actual process of change into consideration. They don't help you take the necessary steps to become and remain committed to change, seeing it through from start to finish.

Introduction to the S.H.I.F.T. Model™

The first step in the S.H.I.F.T. Model™ is **Specifying the Desired Outcome**. In businesses, managers frequently assume everyone on staff knows where the company is headed. When we survey employees, however, we often find they have a great deal of confusion about where the company is going and what it is trying to achieve.

The first step in the change model picks up on this principle. It always starts with defining exactly what the company or team is trying to accomplish. Many times I find a lack of response or clarity about what success really means. Defining the goal carefully and with exactitude is the first crucial step in any change effort.

The second step in the process is to **Highlight and Categorize the Obstacles to Change**. This process of clearly and deliberately identifying obstacles is important to uncover what is or may be standing between where you are with your business and where you want it to be.

I often see businesses assuming that they will just forge ahead and tackle whatever gets in their way. Then they find the same obstacles rearing up again and again and their resolve, their commitment to change, starts to diminish.

Defining the obstacles beforehand, though, lets you capture and categorize what you must plan for ahead of time. It also lets you identify those things that are out of your control, so you don't waste your resources and time worrying about them.

Although we'll talk about how to highlight and categorize obstacles later, when it comes to categories, you're generally going to find things like cost, time, availability of resources, and business rivals and competitors to be the most significant types of obstacles. For instance, if your goal is to enter into a new market—thereby expanding your company, increasing your profit margins, etc.—you will probably find that there are potential obstacles that include costs such as researching the new market, bringing a new product line or service to market, or putting together a team to achieve the work to successfully target the new market; or there could be time factors such as a limited time window in which you have a reasonable chance of being successful before the competition gets there; or perhaps availability of resources, such as the necessary technology for the development of a compelling product/service offering. Some obstacles fall into the category of things you may not be able to directly control, such as the activities of your competitors. The important thing for a business is that, in advance of implementing the change or initiative, they identify the obstacles and create plans that work around or remove them.

Here's a quick example of a company that successfully categorized obstacles in its planning phase: JetBlue.

After spending about $32 million on their marketing and internal branding, JetBlue has boasted one of the best seat-sales percentages in the U.S. airline business. They have also maintained a high level of customer loyalty. The company seems to have set out to achieve these goals from the first—to be a top airline, highly regarded by customers. In a paper by marketing consultant Tim Leberecht called "True Blue," he cites another goal as being able to maintain a high level of productivity. Unit labor costs in 2003 were reported as 1.9 cents per ASM (available seat mile), which compared with 4.4 cents for Delta Airlines.

Assessing the obstacles to operating as a successful airline, however, the company identified obstacles such as cost, customer loyalty (or rather, disloyalty), and low productivity/high operating costs.

To overcome these obstacles, JetBlue set out to offer a particularly clear pricing system—customers know what they are paying for, and costs are made clear, and consequently controlled. Most tickets are bought online and there is an emphasis on online marketing and sales to support this, helping to keep operating costs for the company down to a minimum level, although tickets can also be bought at a call center.

Cutting the cost of paper, postage, employee time, and back-office processing, the company also made its lowest fares available on the website. Keeping advertising costs to a minimum, the company undertook a great deal of its marketing through word-of-mouth campaigning. Consumers were encouraged to recommend the company to friends, and thus JetBlue only applied modest advertising and public relations to supplement the word-of-mouth efforts.

Conducting their assessment of obstacles types, they identified a key area that was holding the company back overall. Communication was the main issue. Employees were reluctant to communicate, and this translated into a limited trust in the organization.

Based on a subsequent review of these obstacles, the company implemented a plan for, as the slogan expresses, "Bringing humanity back into the airline industry," emphasizing communication between the company and its customers, and internally, within the company. The process of setting the objectives, knowing what they were doing well but identifying the obstacles to future success, allowed them to figure out plans that addressed that obstacle in particular. If JetBlue hadn't been proactive in this area, it might have hurt them as they continued to grow. Instead, this became a leverage point for them.

Once you are successful in identifying and categorizing obstacles to your plans for change, the third step in the shift model is to **Identify the Human Factor** and to take into account all human-related elements in your planning and goal achievement process.

This step looks at behavioral style, how we all tend to take a different approach to problem solving and communication, and how these different approaches can hamper our ability to connect and work together most effectively. The human factor step requires introspection, but it also requires us to look outward to see who else in our universe will have an impact on our decisions. This step looks at the issues individuals have within an organization that might hold them back or give them an advantage in a particular area, and it also looks at the stakeholders in any company or on a team that can impact—for better or for worse—a change process.

Once the first three steps are completed, the model moves to **Finding Alternatives**. Finding alternatives can be fun and it often allows creativity to flow. To make the process practical and workable, though, this step should only be taken after other steps have been completed. It's hard to know what options you have until you have clearly specified your goal, your obstacles, and the human factors you will encounter in your change process.

The last step in the model is to **Take Disciplined Action**, and it is with this step that you get to create your specific plan in a methodical fashion. It changes the too-common dynamic of having an "idea," talking about it, planning for it, and thinking about it for a long time — but never doing anything. Instead, using this last step, we know what we need to do and we can construct a very clear plan to get us there. This is where project management skills, defining time lines, considering who and how much, and other important factors must be considered and identified.

As you work your way through this book, working on each of these steps, tailored to your business, keep in mind that businesses have been using the S.H.I.F.T. Model™ in their work with me for years. They've used it without knowing what it was called, without necessarily knowing the names of each individual step. The point is to look beyond the nametags, beyond the basics of each step, and see what it is that the step sets out to achieve. The SHIFT Model™ is a process that works if you are prepared to recognize the fundamental principles upon which it is based.

"Sometimes, we just don't know enough about what we are trying to achieve."
—Stuart Wilde

CHAPTER 1

Specify Your Desired Outcome

A s human beings, we are programmed a certain way. Most of us, to get motivated and to stay motivated, need to focus on an end goal that is truly meaningful. Much of the time, this principle translates, in a business setting, to the suggestion that a business plan is fundamental to change, that an organization needs to know where it's going before it can make a meaningful journey.

For instance, it is not enough to decide that you want to start a business. You can't actually go into business if this is as far as you get in the planning process. Similarly, you wouldn't complete a college education without knowing what degree you were going to receive and why you wanted that particular degree. We don't do many things in life without having some sense of why we are doing them. And yet, when it comes to the things that matter, most businesses don't take the time to think deeply and paint a picture of what they really want.

It's not enough to decide that you want to start a business or that you want to try a new marketing strategy. You need to know what business you want to be in, and you need a reason for being in that business.

Depending on the firm—what it does, how it's run—the desired outcomes will be very different and, in many cases, will actually drive the culture and values of the firm. Ben & Jerry's is a company that stands out for its effective communication of the company goal with just about every individual who works there. When Ben Cohen and Jerry Greenfield opened their first ice cream shop in 1977, they set their desired outcome to create something different. They hoped to establish a profitable business, but they also hoped to make a positive impact on the world.

With these goals in mind, Ben & Jerry, as they would so famously become known, wanted to give something back to their community—so they began by throwing a local festival and giving away free ice cream cones to people who attended.

When their business expanded, they also expanded their efforts to keep up with their goal of giving back to society. They donated an unparalleled percentage of profits to charity, formed partnerships with minority suppliers, and developed environment-friendly packaging.

Their level of social responsibility shaped all other aspects of their business, too, from product development to marketing to human resources to operations. Company leaders were always guided in their decision-making by the social impact of their efforts.

The story of Ben & Jerry's devotion to social causes is something that is shared with everyone who works for the company, so that they understand where the company has come from and where it is heading. The company's desired outcome is very clearly defined and communicated throughout the firm. We could assume that everyone who works there knows what is important and keeps their eye on what matters most.

When a company fails to define its desired outcome, though, that doesn't mean they don't think about the future, or that they haven't thought about it. Most companies set their business objectives and identify the performance expectations for each individual. But too many times businesses don't really focus on what success looks like to them — the desired outcome they have for the activities they are doing, what constitutes the broader picture.

And in too many cases, companies don't tend to look at "cause and effect" in goal setting. For example, as a business owner if I set a goal that says "I want to turn a million-dollar profit this year," is that really the sum and substance of my company's objectives? If I reached the million-dollar level, will I be able to consider my firm successful? If I'm honest, I might see that there are other components that also matter to me. What if one of my key employees, someone whose efforts could be integral to the achievement of this objective, has an illness and is unable to work for a period of time? Would I also want to be a firm that shows care and compassion for my employees as we work toward the million-dollar mark?

Or what about engaging in charitable endeavors, because I care about my community and want to have a presence in my local market? Perhaps my business is a cutting-edge technology firm and I also care about product and development and designing new advancements in technology.

If I state my overall goal only in the quantitative terms of the profit I am striving for — as many firms tend to do — I miss out on other aspects of what kind of firm I want to have, and how I want my firm to be known. In many, many companies we've worked with, employees may know there is a profit or revenue goal, but they don't know why that goal was set and they don't know what else is important to the firm's success.

Capturing desired outcomes using the S.H.I.F.T. Model™ approach means looking more holistically at the company's, or the team's, objectives. When a goal is more traditionally set in a vacuum, it's likely that the goal will be met—but something else may be sacrificed in the process.

Cause and Effect

To illustrate how the traditional goal-setting process can actually hamper our efforts, I'll share a personal story in the development of my career. I had been taught to look at the different segments of my life—work, family, spiritual, hobbies, etc.—and to set goals for each one individually. Before I fully grasped the importance of clearly defining what success meant to me by looking at the overall impact on my life, I made the mistake of taking steps in a particular direction, toward a general goal, without realizing how one area actually blended into another. In this case, I wanted to be a popular public speaker, and I set a goal of wanting to be paid to speak all across the country on topics that I really enjoyed. When I set this goal, however, I didn't think about the impact it would have on my family. I didn't think about how much I would miss my children, or about the physical wear and tear I'd have to endure, traveling around the country. I found myself being wildly successful and in demand all over the country, getting paid to speak in many different forums on topics I enjoyed. So, I reached the goal I had set and I technically should have been happy as a result. But I realized that I couldn't fully enjoy my success because I also gave up so much; because I didn't take the time to clearly define my desired outcome overall for my life and establish what success would mean to me in that context. If I had looked at my overall desired outcome, and all of the components of who I am and what matters to me, I would have realized that I was missing key ingredients of my definition of "success" and what would make me happy.

This is not an uncommon situation for professionals or businesses. Business owners and managers often get fixated on a goal or focus on one thing that they dream of achieving with their company. This goal becomes the most important thing, and sometimes the sole focus, and everyone drives toward the goal. But once the goal is met, the company may also learn they've given up something in the process. For example, a firm we worked with was very determined to cut their costs. They had a stated goal of "cutting overall budget by 15% of current operating costs." This goal became a rallying cry throughout the organization, and everyone knew the firm was striving toward this objective. While they reached the objective, the mess that was created was significant: Very unhappy customers based upon cutbacks they'd made. Employees who felt they were undervalued and overworked, and who started to abandon the firm. And, in the most extreme case, a contract with a disaster recovery vendor that went unsigned because it was considered too expensive (but no alternative was determined) and difficulties arose when the company had an emergency situation and no vendor in place to back them up.

This is an example of how being laser-focused on one singular goal, without considering what else matters to the firm—the holistic approach—can have unexpected and unintended negative consequences.

But many firms, such as Ben & Jerry's for example, know there are components to what's important to their overall success. They consider all of the pieces and create a desired outcome that is more comprehensive. Let's look at another example of a business that did a great job of setting specific goals for their firm.

An investment advisor client of ours was interested in growing his business by focusing on client referrals. While he had very satisfied clients, they were not referring to the extent that he needed—or felt was warranted. However, in many cases obtaining client referrals means holding events, spending more one-to-one time with clients, and the like. This advisor had young children and said, "While I care about growth in my firm, and I want to increase my client referrals by 25% over the current level, I also want to be able to stop working at 2 p.m. every Friday so I can pick my kids up from school and spend the rest of the afternoon with them. Managing my time effectively and being as efficient as I can be is equally as important to me as the number of increased referrals."

In addition, he said, "I only want to work with a certain kind of client. I don't feel that everyone is a good fit for me, and in fact some clients are draining to me. I want to become more focused on the kind of people that I actually can enjoy working with in my practice."

Setting this goal with specific parameters meant that simply creating programs and events to obtain additional client referrals wasn't going to work; the question became how to do this most efficiently—quality over quantity—and how to attract the right kinds of people. Having a more well-rounded goal that looked at the desire to increase client referrals coupled with his personal desires around time led him to develop an approach that focused on the combined, overall desired outcome. He was able to utilize online webinars, social media, and video on his website to reach out to clients. He developed a message and a story that made it clear to prospects whom he felt he could help and who would be a good fit with his firm. To be more efficient with existing and new clients, he also set up a recorded conference call speaking about his expertise and what he was doing for clients. Clients were able to access his expertise, share it with friends, and introduce his firm to others more easily. He exceeded his goal of 25% new referrals working mostly with the kind of people he really enjoyed, but all along he was also finding ways to be much more efficient. After several months, this led to his ability to take off the entire Friday once a month and leave at 2 p.m. on the other days.

This is not an unusual outcome when the leader, or the management, is willing to take the time to consider all of the aspects of what's important. In my consulting experience, working with businesses from very small to very large, I've learned the importance of looking at the whole picture and understanding exactly what individuals or businesses want — and why they want it.

The problem with classic goal setting, as most of us have come to understand it, is that the goals tend to be formulated in a vacuum. Even when we go through the motions of writing a business plan to outline our goals and we try to set SMART goals, we follow the same process to pick our goals. We have a desire, we set the goal, and then we put steps in place to help us meet that goal. We don't think about the "why," even though businesses have a variety of dynamics that are at play each and every day.

When we set goals that say only that we need to reach that particular objective, we are missing a large piece of the overall puzzle. Instead of classic goal setting, we need to paint a picture of what success looks like in its entirety. What does success look like to your firm?

Multiple Facets of Defining the Goal

Businesses have many facets associated with what they do. Classic goal setting will tell you to categorize these and set goals in each category — financial goals, team goals, growth goals, etc.

In a business, it's often the case that one area will set a goal that will actually conflict with another area in the company. People within a company often don't work together; instead, they work at odds with one another, and the business managers can't understand why the company doesn't have a team culture.

For instance, a company with multiple departments could have its human resource department looking to cut costs by modifying pay structures for employees in its research and development (R & D) department while—at the same time—its R & D department is looking to research the possible development of a new product or product line. The two objectives could end up being in conflict. The one calls for cutbacks and downsizing, while the other calls for investment in research and certainly suggests the need for employees to work more hours, not fewer. If employees in R & D are worried about cutbacks and the stability of their salary or their role, asking them to be results-focused and "go the extra mile" is going to fall on deaf ears. But management wants the department to meet the aggressive R & D goal, and perhaps there is a sales team that is already out pre-selling the new product. In cases like this, it's a common outcome that a business will actually find departments pitted against one another in some way, because the goals are not in alignment with an overall comprehensive goal. This leads to loss of focus, loss of time, and loss of energy, and is detrimental to the overall organization.

As a senior manager in my corporate career, I am well aware that at times it may actually be necessary to have competing goals between different departments and units. But, if the business takes the time and defines its overall desired outcome, it will have to look at the impact of these competing objectives and consider whether there is a resulting loss to the firm. I believe the best goal setting looks at the entire picture at the outset and identifies all of the components of what is most important.

When helping teams to craft their overall desired outcome, I often use an analogy in these corporate settings. I ask them to think about a Jenga™ tower—the game where you pull out one piece at a time, hoping the whole tower won't come falling down on your turn. I ask them to think about pulling out one piece of the overall tower—it's possible that the tower will keep standing, but it's also possible that if you pull the wrong piece, the whole thing will come crashing down. This is what scattershot decision-making and having goals in a vacuum can do to a business, and it's what often creates the "fire drill" mentality: We fix one thing only to have to turn our attention to fixing something else.

Looking at your overall desired outcome—what you want your business to look like once you achieve the goal you are striving toward—asks you to take into account all of the pieces that matter to you. At this stage, you certainly want to identify single, specific goals, but you also want your final desired outcome to be a comprehensive, clear, and understandable overall definition of what success looks like to your team or your firm.

Working with another business client of mine recently, I was reminded again of how simple this step seems to be and yet how difficult it is to put into practice. I was working with a team of people who were not meeting their goals, and feeling so frustrated about it that they were beginning to turn on each other. I was called in to help them improve their performance.

Before I started the meeting, I asked them first to define success for our meeting and then for the overall goal they were hoping to accomplish as a team. What would the desired outcome look like to them at the end of our hours spent together? What was their desired outcome for the issues we were trying to resolve? How would they know in one year if we made changes that worked well for them? I posed the question I often ask, "What would success look like to this team if everything was as you'd like it to be one year from now?"

They clearly defined their objectives for our meeting, which allowed us to stay on track with our discussions. Thinking about the longer-term desired outcome, the results were interesting — while they wanted to reach the quantitative goals that had been set by the company, it was just as important to them that they work together more effectively. Things like "We will be listening more acutely and respecting one another's opinion" were high on their list.

It can be difficult to define what "listening more acutely" really means, so as part of the exercise to specify the desired outcome we had to identify what was happening now and what they wanted to happen in the future. Things like team members not interrupting one another, engaging in reflective listening and feeding back understanding, and each person having a voice during a meeting were all identified as part of the desired outcome. The "soft component," as it is sometimes called, can be hard to define, but people do have an idea of what that portion of success looks like to them. What's important in this first step is taking the time to dissect and capture each component clearly, so we know if we've met the goal in its entirety. They also added that they'd like to be having fun. They wanted to be successful in the eyes of their firm, but they cared about the team dynamics. They wanted to be respectful of one another, and enjoy what they were doing each day. The picture they painted of success included many aspects that were important to each of them as individuals, to the team overall, and to the company they were working for.

This meeting was precipitated by the need to "make the numbers," but when we finished writing the goal, the final desired outcome their team sought was much deeper than that. If the only relevant measurement of success was meeting the numbers, the way they interacted would never have entered into the equation and they certainly wouldn't have talked about "fun." Chances are they would be in the same place next year, or more likely they would have met the revenue objective but have had difficulties working with one another. This is an example of why focusing on just one aspect won't help you attain even that limited goal without sacrificing something else in the process, and why for businesses, looking at all of the pieces at the outset can save a great deal of time, money, and aggravation throughout the goal achievement process.

The Why Behind the What

Before you begin to record your desired outcome, think about the components that matter to your team or your firm. For example, if you want to develop an online aspect of your business, ask yourself why you want to go online—what prompted you to determine this as an objective? Is it because you have identified that there is a sizeable market for taking your business online? Have you had customers ask you about whether you have a website, whether they can place orders online? Are your competitors making the move? Are you perhaps losing business to companies that operate exclusively online, with low overheads and lower prices?

Or perhaps you want to open a new business location. Why? Has your company grown to such a point that it makes sense to target a new location outside of your main area? Are your competitors gaining ground in an area where you do not have a presence? Perhaps your management team feels a different location would offer more prestige to your firm. It's not that there's a right or wrong answer about why the company may choose to strive in a certain direction, or set a particular objective. What matters is thinking about the reasons you have set this goal and understanding more about what's driving your decision to focus in any given area.

Think about why you want to set each of the goals you have for your business. What is the real reason for what you are trying to do? In the teambuilding example, it turned out that the purpose of meeting together was not just to figure out how to reach a sales goal. Behind that goal lay the fact that they were tired of fighting with one another and they wanted to enjoy their work lives a little more. And they were afraid—afraid of what might happen if they didn't meet their goals. Every time we have a desire, something we wish to do, there is an underlying "why" behind it. When a company says to their employees, "We want to be at $2 million in revenue at this time next year," you can be assured that the employees are asking "Why?" What is the reason for that number? Is it necessary for the company to meet budget? Is it the perceived opportunity in the market? Where did that number come from?

Let's consider the case of a company that set the goal of establishing an online aspect to the business. Why are they going online at this particular time? Why not last year or next year? What's prompting the move in this direction? And what are the specific objectives to be pursued in this online component? How will the company define success? What kind of quantifiable and qualitative goals will be assigned to this objective? Ask the question, "What will success look like to you?" If the online aspect is deemed successful, what does that really mean—detail and define it. Sometimes I ask clients to paint a verbal picture of what it will look like if they reach the success they desire. What's happening with this online aspect of the business if you are successful? What's it contributing to your firm overall? What kind of people within your firm are managing it or working there? How will it integrate with and impact your other brick and mortar aspect to the business? Will they complement one another or will it shift from one delivery method to another?

As you can begin to see by the questions we ask, the key to setting specific goals and being able to explain them is perhaps most obviously to know the situation with which you are dealing. You need to understand the context in which you are looking to make a shift. Think of it as a gear shift or a lane shift driving on a highway. You have to look all around you before you make a move into a new lane. You must examine how the conditions around you, everything from the weather to the traffic, are going to affect how you make the shift in speed or direction. Your goal and the trigger that compels you to make the shift to achieve the goal will also become crucial in determining exactly what you do. If your goal is to speed up so you can get to your destination faster, your shift will reflect the best way to avoid obstacles that will slow you down and the best way to drive as quickly as possible, without breaking the speed limit or putting yourself in unnecessary danger. If you know you need to change your position—change lanes, so you can prepare for a turn off the highway—again, the shift you make is going to be different, dependent upon how the surrounding circumstances affect you. When you're making a shift with your business, the same principles apply.

© Randy Glasbergen
www.glasbergen.com

"**Success is where preparation and opportunity meet.
Failure is where they meet, but can't stand each other.**"

In our previous example, the business looking to branch into the online world needs to understand what they are out to achieve, and it's got to be more than "set up a website" or "develop an online presence." This is exactly how most goals are stated in many businesses. But it's important to also ask: What is the purpose of the online presence, the website? The principal answer, put succinctly, could be "to sell to more customers." The answer might also cover points such as "take advantage of the added convenience or flexibility for customers (being able to buy things online, not having to run to the store all the time, being able to price shop can be a real blessing)." In essence, though, in this example the reason is mostly about selling to customers. So if this is the main driver behind the desired outcome, the firm will want to expand on how they will be using the web to sell to customers: what percentage of business they expect will come in from this channel, what web presence they want to have, etc.

In the 21st century, many businesses are finding it necessary to have some online presence and to target online customers if for no other reason that it opens up a phenomenal range of opportunities, and affords the potential for lower overheads, greater flexibility in marketing (traditional marketing equals high costs, limited effectiveness), and a potentially unlimited market. But just wanting to jump on the bandwagon and participate in the wave isn't enough. It's about knowing what the online world means to you, for your business and your objectives; defining clearly and specifically what your desired outcome is for this aspect of your business.

To set a desired outcome, first think about what's creating your desire to make a shift. Record what triggered you to consider reading this book — what's happening that prompts you to want to make a shift within your team or within your firm. You want to take a minute to identify what is happening that you'd like to change. Put this book down now and record what you hoped to gain by reading this book and learning this process to apply in your firm.

As you take a minute in the process to record this, think also about what is likely to happen if you don't make a shift with the company. Where will you be if things don't change for you and you don't make any movement at all toward your desired outcome? Identifying this helps us more fully understand the why of what we want to do, and helps us to clarify where we need to shift.

In the case above of a business branching out online, if the shift is not made, it's likely that the company, by sticking to a traditional, brick and mortar business, would lose some portion of its customers over time to those businesses that do manage to offer a website, online ordering, and the like. The trigger for the desired shift might even be the specific successes of a competitor working online or with social media. While your competitor may be seizing an opportunity and doing it effectively, you may be falling behind in market share. Whatever the nature of your business, take advantage of the questions below to start thinking about the reasons for the goals and objectives you are setting for your business:

- What is prompting the organization/team/division to seek this goal/desired outcome?
- Why is it so important to achieve this goal at this point?
- What would happen if the organization/team/division didn't identify this goal?
- What are the facets to this goal? Are there multiple aspects and if so, what are each of them as listed individually?
- Do any of our individual (i.e., personal or departmental) goals conflict with other goals?

Moving Toward? Or Away From?

Once you know where you are with your business and what's triggered you to set the goals you have in sight, you can start to create an impression of where you want to be with your business in a kind of end-stage.

So, for example, let's say you're tired of seeing problems with your customer service and your staff's handling of customer complaints. A typical goal would be "to set up a successful customer service program." But it is important to be much more specific and clear about the desired outcome. You have to look at why customer service is such an important component in your business, and what has prevented it from being successful in the past. Why is it at this point that you want to try and implement a clear and effective policy to handle this aspect of the business, and how will you benefit from the pursuit of this goal?

There are two basic reasons we move in a new direction: Either we are looking to move toward something new and positive, or our goal is to move away from something that is negative, that is disliked or ineffective. As the best salespeople know, both are motivators and both will urge us to action. But when we are moving away from something, we want to have a clear view of what's next—what's the outcome we hope for when we get where we want to go? This is important because oftentimes businesses and people try and move away from situations or things they don't like, only to end up in a situation that is no better. Consider what is motivating you—dig down to uncover the reasons behind your desire to shift to this goal. Consider how you and your company are actually going to benefit.

Once you have identified what's driving the goal, you can begin to clarify the desired outcome. All of this is rather like managing a construction project. You need to know what you're working with, what resources and what limitations; you need blueprints to govern how you proceed, you need systems to manage your work, and in the end, of course, you still have to review and possibly continue to revise your work.

As you look at the answers to why you want to pursue a particular goal, though, and what's creating the desire for the shift it represents, you may uncover more specifics about what's important to your organization. So now, instead of "set up a customer service program," you might have revised it to something like: "Establish a dedicated customer service department that costs the firm no more than 10% of last year's revenue to set up that will allow more effective handling of customers' needs and allow the general staff to function more effectively and specifically as a sales team."

Maybe you are looking to address your employees' general dislike toward handling customers with problems. Perhaps your employees are struggling with both small customer service issues (such as irritated customers that employees didn't know how to deal with when they called) and larger problems, such as belligerent dissatisfaction on the part of most of your customer base. As you set the desired outcome and talk with your staff about the why and the different components you may, on the other hand, find that the real objectives are more about finding ways to help your staff function more effectively, helping their work for the company to be more clearly defined. Having staff struggle to manage customer complaints and provide customer service may have precipitated the company's desire to shift, but maybe it wasn't the real reason behind the final outcome you are seeking.

If your goal is simply to allow your employees to avoid dealing with customers, dealing with problems, then the company is unlikely to address the underlying issue—the need for a dedicated customer service department. In addition, you don't want a customer service department at any cost; your firm has identified that you can invest 10% of last year's revenue to establish this. This allows you, and the team creating this department, to also have a financial target and make smart decisions in hiring and funding the initiative. If you're making a meaningless shift, that's all you will get; you'll get more of the same — an expensive effort that involves a bunch of employees dealing with the same problems and being no happier about what they are doing!

Once you look at all of the pieces, and can create a clear and multi-faceted scenario like this with a lot more detail to illustrate what's important to you, you can navigate with more confidence toward what you want. Writing the entire scenario as the desired outcome has now become a first step. As you move toward your shift, you will be able to check in with your desired outcome to make sure that where you are headed includes all the different components of what's important to you.

The Why Behind the What

Understanding the "why" behind what we want can help us to more deeply crystallize what it is we're really after.

Before you firmly set your goal, it may be necessary, and it is certainly important, to do a bit of soul searching to find what's driving your desire for change. This applies to companies, to individuals, and to teams. For a company it could be that we want to increase market share. But why? What's important about market share? It will bring us more money? It will edge out competitors? We are losing market share now? What do we think increasing our market share will do for us?

We need to understand the "why" behind our desires so we can ensure that we are focused on the right things, that we have the right motivations, and that when we reach the goal we'll have accomplished whatever underlying desires prompted us to seek it out in the first place. Once when I was going through this process with a client and I kept asking them for more clarification on the desired outcome, she finally turned to me and asked, "So you really want me to solve the right problem instead of just the problem I think is most important to me?" And that about summed it up—we can spend a lot of time and energy trying to get somewhere, but unless we're very careful in analyzing where we want to go, we might arrive at the place we set out for and realize it isn't where we want to be at all, and that it doesn't really shift us from our current state in a real and lasting way.

Let's look at a goal of starting a social media campaign for a company. If you consider the motivations of most companies in starting social media campaigns, you'll notice they are often not only acting out of a desire to improve their marketing by taking advantage of a compelling marketing option, they are also looking to experiment and ultimately cut advertising costs. This is important, because a singular focus in planning, without considering other aspects of your business needs that are equally important, leads to the "be careful what you wish for" problem. You could end up changing the way your company operates, how it's branded, by focusing exclusively on a social media-driven campaign. If you focus on cutting advertising costs without really considering other means of getting your message out there that will allow your firm to be more effective, you could end up cutting costs and little else. The effectiveness of your marketing will not necessarily be increased; indeed, it might become less effective.

Even when you're focused on business goals and change, you don't want to give up something that is important to your company in favor of something else, unless your priorities have truly shifted and other things don't matter to you. This change in priority can happen with life changes; for example, when one CEO steps down and is replaced by another, or when a business gets rid of a certain line of products. The things that matter to us do change over time, but we need to take into account everything that currently matters to us when we are hoping to move to a new place. To simply "trade" one important priority for another rarely brings us the overall success for our firm and the happiness we are hoping to achieve.

Begin to look at your business and goal setting differently — hopefully you can see how classic goal setting can be too linear an approach. You may get something you want, but sacrifice something else meaningful in the process. You may move away from something you don't like, but find you are somewhere new that isn't much better than what you left behind.

Consider All Aspects

As I said earlier, considering my own example of wanting to do more public speaking, a phenomenon I've noticed over the years is that in our goal setting we are rarely aware of, or at least rarely focus on, the fact that when we define something we are striving for, it may actually be in conflict with something else in our lives that is important. In one case, a technology company I was consulting with had a goal of achieving a certain percentage increase in sales of a certain software product line. They communicated this goal to their sales and client service troops, changed the compensation structure to favor sales of this product line, and put on client and prospect training events focused on the product line. They were entirely focused on their goal for this product and felt they had taken all of the necessary steps to achieve the right outcome. When I came to work with them, they were baffled by the fact that their sales reps were selling only the new product line and not any of the other products!

Because of their singular focus on the one product line, they were actually blinded to the negative impact on other product areas.

Without considering an overall desired outcome, they got the product as a featured sale but unwittingly sacrificed other products in the process. Their desired outcome really needed to include the entire vision of the company, including other product lines. For example, their goal could have been stated as such: "We want the company to grow by X% overall and we want this particular product line to be our leading product, accounting for 25% of our overall goal." This newly revised goal would leave 75% of the total revenue coming from other products, but still give a significant stake to the product they want their sales force focused on. In this goal, they aren't trading one thing for another, but rather encompassing all of what is important to the company's success.

This approach allows you to keep more than one thing in front of you as you forge toward a goal. Think of it as incorporating both the quantitative (the actual percentage of growth you want to see) and qualitative (focusing the direction of the company in the way that is most meaningful for you) aspects of what matters to the organization.

This approach works well but is underused in business. For example, take a firm that is struggling to achieve a monetary goal of $2 million this year. The management puts forth this revenue number at all costs, but then discovers that the employees are miserably unhappy and aren't working together effectively. The solution is for the business to include all of the aspects that are important and then state the desired outcome, including everything they need to achieve — without sacrificing one goal for another. It's not mutually exclusive to both achieve impressive revenue goals and have happy, team-oriented employees working together to get there. In fact, many very successful firms have both — because they set their desired outcomes to include the monetary and the people aspects, instead of simply focusing on only one or the other.

Put it in Writing!

Taking the time and being crystal clear in identifying, in writing, your desired outcome keeps you on track once you finally create the plan for your business (the last step in the S.H.I.F.T. Model™). Have you ever set out to do something with your business and then found you were wasting time on something else? Many businesses don't record what they desire and don't set the priorities associated with the desired outcome. As a result, time gets wasted on activities that don't lead to the ultimate goal.

As a leader of a firm spending time in less productive activities, you might find yourself frustrated and wanting to turn your attention back to your important goal, but you were so engaged in the other thing that you couldn't do it! I've found this to happen with many of the executives that I coach. We may start the week out with a clear set of desired outcomes, but then when we time-track at the end of the week, the time has been spent in other areas.

When that happens, I need to ask, "Is this objective really that important to you?" Things that aren't really priorities and that won't lead to the ultimate goal will end up getting in the way, and the person I am working with may start to feel frustrated that they haven't made the progress they desire.

Having a clearly defined set of success objectives for your business can help you decide what you and your employees or coworkers, your fellow stakeholders, should spend time on. After all, it's easy to get distracted and spend your time and energy on things that aren't really high-gain activities. Think about how we can get distracted just sitting at a desk; by reading funny emails, or by visiting a social media site, or by chatting on the phone with someone for a long period of time. Not that any of these things are wrong, but you want to be sure to do them only when you have the time, and you want to make sure they are not taking away from your ultimate goal. It's

Worksheet 1: Specify Your Outcome

What is the desired outcome for my team/division/organization?

How do we define success?

What are the quantifiable (measurable) aspects of the specific goal?

What are the qualitative aspects of the goal?

When we do expect (or need) to meet this goal?

What don't we want to sacrifice in meeting this goal?

a matter of keeping all the pieces in place and not trading one for another. Keeping focused on your outcome actually makes your life a bit easier, because it's easier to allocate time if your desired outcome is in front of you and everyone else in your organization at all times. The question is no longer a broad-based question of what you should be doing; now it's a question of what will move you closer to your goal most efficiently. It gets easier to say "no" to distractions or things that don't matter as much.

As you've read this chapter, hopefully you've had a chance to think more clearly about what you are really looking for in your business shift. Before you move on to the next step, use the worksheet on page 37 to record your desired outcome in its entirety — the place you want to shift to in your company, or a particular aspect of your company. These can be smaller business goals like spending more public relations time on social media, or they can be much larger objectives around shifting the competitive position of the company, bringing out a new product line, or targeting a new market with a new range of services.

Be sure to reflect back to when you stated the "why" of this goal and what matters to you about it now.

The SMART Goal-Setting Process

You may still be having a hard time understanding all of the ways to think about your desired outcome. If so, try jogging your thinking by using SMART goal setting. We mentioned SMART goals a bit earlier although, by itself, the SMART approach to goal setting, while widely used, is often not enough. SMART goals, however, are worth using as part of a more comprehensive approach. The approach was invented by George Doran, Arthur Miller, and James Cunningham, who wrote an article about goal setting in 1981. This well-known approach to arriving at a goal is taught in many colleges and used by many businesses, and I use it in the Leadership course I teach to illustrate how to break down a goal when someone is struggling to fully define their desired outcome.

The five SMART criteria are: The goal must be specific, measurable, actionable, realistic, and time-bound. You may want to go back and review your desired outcome and make sure it's specified clearly in terms of an overall desired outcome, and not just a simply stated goal. See if it's measurable. If you look back at the examples in this chapter, you'll find that there are always numeric and quantitative components that can be measured. If there aren't measurements built in, it may be hard to know if you have reached the success you desired. "Actionable" and "realistic" means that you know what you need to do to get the goal accomplished, and that it is a feasible goal. For example, if you are currently breaking even with your business and you set a desired outcome to turn a million-dollar profit next year, it might not be a very realistic goal given other factors in your business or in your industry. Finally, time-bound means defining when you want to reach this goal. "Launching a social media campaign at some point" could mean next month or it could mean 15 years from now, and it's crucial to know which. I've seen many companies set the same goal year after year because they haven't identified a specific point in time—a certain date—they want to accomplish something. We'll take a closer look at this when we get to the last step: taking disciplined action and identifying how you will actually accomplish your shift—the what, the when, the who in detail for your plan.

Before you read on, take the time to answer the questions posed in this chapter and capture what your desired outcome entails, why it is important to you and to your organization, and what quantifiable and qualitative measures you will use to know when you have achieved it.

Following Todd Galant

Todd called us to work with his firm when he had hired and then lost the fourth person for a single position in two years. He realized how much money he was losing by churning people through the position. When he came to us, he asked, "Can you help me find a good person for this role?" Before we began, we asked him to define the desired outcome. What did a "good person" really mean to him? Was any good person going to be a good fit? What else did he care about? As we went through this process, Todd began to uncover other aspects of the situation that mattered to him. He ended up with the following desired outcome: "To find a seasoned professional with experience in our industry to fill the role of Consulting Liaison within the next four months. This person will be a cultural fit with our firm and will be motivated, proactive, and engaged. He or she will be able to hit the ground running and instead of seeking direction, will give input and ideas to make the role take shape. The person will be hired by a collaborative decision reached by the five identified members of the firm."

Todd's final desired outcome much more clearly stated exactly what he needed—not just a "good person" as he had started out to find—and it also clarified how he would go about identifying the right person throughout the process.

"Sometimes the situation is only a problem because it is looked at in a certain way. Looked at in another way, the right course of action may be so obvious that the problem no longer exists."
—*Edward de Bono*

CHAPTER 2

Highlight and Categorize Your Obstacles

Most of us have heard Rita Mae Brown's definition of "insanity" — doing the same thing over and over again but expecting a different result. But even though we intuitively understand the insanity, we stay insane too much of the time. For instance, we have the same fights with people, we engage in the same futile activities, we put the same ineffective plans into place, but somehow we think that this time we'll get a different outcome from using the same approach. And then of course we are disappointed with ourselves and with our results because, yet again, something didn't work.

Many a person or organization has set out with the best of intentions, only to be thwarted by some unforeseen (or foreseen) obstacle in the way. It's not that you shouldn't take on aggressive goals. The point is that the realities of life will kick in for each of us on our way to our goals, and if we haven't identified those realities we are not giving ourselves a chance to succeed.

What Stands in the Way?

Obstacles are those things that stand in our way — the problems, the issues, the difficulties our business has already encountered, or may at some point encounter. Highlighting obstacles can be difficult, because most people don't like to be complainers and they often don't want to focus on what is, or might be, a problem somehow. Many organizations don't want to "open a can of worms" by asking their staff what's working and what's not.

The leader who is an optimist will say, "Why look at the problems? We'll just forge through and figure it out as we go along!" while the pessimistic employee might say, "Once I realize how much is in my way, I lose my motivation to do anything!"

Both sides are missing an important part of the equation. In my career, for instance, I have lost count of the number of managers or leaders who are reluctant to talk about obstacles. They already know what the obstacles are, they insist. What they want to find out is how to fix things! "Don't bring me a problem — bring me a solution!" is the most familiar refrain. What these managers misunderstand is the importance of identifying those things that may block the successful accomplishment of the desired outcome. Once identified, it's possible to create a plan that manages around, or completely eliminates, these obstacles.

As a simple example to illustrate the importance of this: If a firm sets out to manufacture a particular product from scratch and they need to have it ready by the end of the week, they will need to start by thinking about how much time is needed to work on it. If they consider only the time necessary to go through the manufacturing process, though, and as such start just a day or so before the work is due, then they surely haven't identified the obstacles properly. Obstacles could include anything from lack of resources such as materials on hand, constraints upon employee time and availability, or other products that are already midway through the process and have all of the equipment geared toward them. It only takes a couple of unexpected obstacles, some issues you haven't anticipated and planned for, and suddenly you're not going to reach your objective within the deadline. Even if you do somehow make the deadline, the effort required might cost a great deal in terms of financial loss, focus in unproductive areas, and management or employee angst! We can certainly push through sometimes by sheer force of will, but we often sacrifice a lot in the process. The cost is felt by organizations as readily as by the individuals forced to work through the obstacles. If you plan for obstacles, however—if you identify them in advance, the process for achieving your goals can be more effective and the experience of undertaking it much less stressful overall.

Does uncovering, identifying, and working through the obstacles sound like a natural and simple process? Perhaps it is—or should be. When I work with people and organizations trying to reach their desired outcomes, though, I see frustration over and over again. Time after time, they express surprise that their well-laid plans have gone awry, when all they really needed to do was spend some time identifying their obstacles and taking them into account in the planning process.

Capture All Obstacles

Once you have finished the first step and set your desired outcome, consider what obstacles have stood in your way in the past and what may derail you in the future from reaching this desired outcome. For example, if your desired outcome is "to establish an online store to support a brick and mortar business within the next six months," some of your obstacles might be as follows:

1. Finding the time to research the online market and how to

target it—employees might already be overstretched.

2. Limited money to invest in the setup and promotion—company will only pay a limited amount for the set-up and considers cost a main priority.

3. When efforts were made in the past to plan an online version of the business, there was, in the end, limited enthusiasm—senior stakeholders in the project have a tendency to procrastinate.

4. Technology related to websites and online stores, online marketing, is constantly changing—keeping up to date is going to take some effort—so you will probably need to have someone tech-savvy on hand, which may mean hiring someone else to join your team.

5. Other objectives within the firm are taking the focus away, and the technology-related staff members are otherwise occupied with other projects that do not have short time frames associated.

This list could be longer, of course, but these are examples of real or potential obstacles. The point of this exercise is not to claim that the desired outcome is not possible and you're doomed to stay in your lowly position forever. That's the last thing I would be trying to communicate in a book about getting the success you desire and deserve! The point is that without identifying what we may have run into in the past, and without knowing what we may run into in the future, there is no way to put together an accurate plan that allows us to work around, or completely remove, the obstacles to our success. In fact, in order to create a workable plan—which is probably your ultimate goal if you are reading this book—you must know what you are up against to plan around and for these obstacles. If you have ever had the situation in your firm, or as a leader of your team, of asking yourself "How did we end up here and why didn't we accomplish what we needed to?" the answer lies in the obstacles that you weren't aware of before you ever started the process.

One of my clients was telling me about an obstacle they were encountering and said, "I told the person in charge of that area, 'just fix it!'" This is a great concept and it sometimes works, but I've found that the obstacle only gets pushed down, waiting to rear up again—because the company hasn't actually solved it. Leaders who want the problem to just go away will find that months and years out, they are still dealing with the same issue in some form or fashion.

While obstacles often stand in our way and prevent us from moving forward, when we recognize what they are and understand them, they can actually give us information about what we need to do to move forward. When talking about this step in the process, I sometimes change the word "obstacles" to "opportunities" because doing so shifts the way I approach them. It's not that we are pretending something that may be difficult is really a great opportunity for us, but the truth is that knowledge is power. Knowing what might stand in the way and being able to see the potential pitfalls in black and white actually gives you the guidance you need to create a plan that either removes or plans around these obstacles. Identifying them does allow the opportunity to plan for and around them. Ignoring them is a lost opportunity.

Granted, the obstacles you face may be significant ones. In business, they could be anything from the lack of time to do the things you want to do to bring about a change, to issues of cost, available resources, issues with employees, etc. But it is critical to bring the obstacles themselves to light even if they can't be turned into opportunities right away. No matter what, finding solutions and making plans becomes easier, not harder, when you know what you might be up against.

Capture, then Categorize

But it's not enough just to list your obstacles. Simply listing them can leave you feeling daunted by the potential trouble you will face trying to succeed. The critical next step, after identifying obstacles, is to categorize them. There are three categories of obstacles: (1) those we can control, (2) those we cannot control but we can influence, and (3) those we cannot control.

As an example, you cannot really control the fact that technology is always changing. You can't control the direction of the changes, the updates that go on with website design and development, online stores, online advertising, and the like. All of this is beyond your control. The best you can hope is that you might end up being able to stay aware and keep up (or nearly keep up) with the changes.

You can, however, take some control over the time that it takes to research the online market and how you manage that process, making it as effective as possible. You cannot necessarily control the funds available to invest in the setup and management, but you can take steps to manage the available funds with maximum efficiency. It might add to your research time to be extremely cost/value conscious, but it is something you can control. You can also manage the lack of enthusiasm felt by your team to a degree as well. You can work to inspire senior stakeholders and implement strategies to help avoid procrastination.

I have gone through this process of discovery with individuals or companies, and I have watched the same scenario unfold many times. The effort will start out with my clients trying to convince me that their "out of our control" problems prevent success. Yet each time, when we list all of the obstacles (and often there are many) and then go through the categorization process, we find that many of the obstacles are in their control after all, or at least within their influence. In life there are really few obstacles we encounter that are completely out of our control—they are there and we need to note them, but only so we don't waste our time trying to go through them instead of around them.

Before we move on to identifying your own obstacles, I want to underscore a problem I notice a lot. In general, we tend to waste a lot of time and energy focusing on those few things that we simply cannot change. We rail and complain and seethe over circumstances and problems that we simply can't solve. I hear people within organizations complain that they can't do what they need to do because of the people in charge. I hear individuals complain that they can't reach their goals because something in their history prevents them from doing so. I hear people in companies I work with at the senior executive level complain that some tax law change will have too much of an impact on their business. In a recent workshop I did with a client, one of the participants at the end—when we asked what they would commit to do differently—raised the fact that he was simply "too busy" to make any changes we had discussed. And yet, this same individual was taking many hours out of his work day to participate in our workshop in the first place! If we value something enough, we'll find a way to work around the obstacle.

To illustrate how the three categories of obstacles work: For example, a new tax law that significantly impacts your business is out of the company's control. The vagaries of the investment market are out of a company's control. In too many cases, the company management spends inordinate amounts of time focusing on the things that are out-of-control obstacles. The energy is spent trying to move things that are actually immovable objects. Trying to move them and wasting time doing so means that a person, or a company, isn't spending that time and energy removing the obstacles they can affect. It's expending resources that could be used in much more productive ways to get stuck on the "can't control" things. These individuals, teams, and leaders within companies are losing their own personal freedom by spending their energy focusing on the "out of my control" obstacles, and organizations lose countless hours in meetings and discussions about those things that can't be controlled.

That's not to say that we don't acknowledge them, or care about them, but placing our focus on this particular segment of obstacles is detrimental overall. Think of the amount of "water cooler talk" that involves the things staff is frustrated about—many organizations have their own gossip component that revolves around frustration with the obstacles. If organizations could leverage productive ways to allow staff and teams to bring the obstacles to light, and then manage them in an effective manner, slowly the obstacles would lose their weight and employees would turn their attention from what they can't do, to what they are doing.

When I coach even senior executives, I set a time limit that we can spend talking about those out-of-control obstacles. It's okay to vent for a short period of time, but then we need to move on to look at what can be controlled and influenced. It's very deflating for the person—and for the company—to get fixated on what can't be fixed!

So how do we bring the obstacles to light to understand what they are and then begin to work through them? Because of the hesitancy on the part of some people to appear to complain, in a group setting if you simply ask the team members "What are we doing wrong?" you may not get a great response. Or the response may feel so overly critical that management puts up a defensive wall that makes it difficult to hear what's really being discussed.

To think about this practically, when I work with teams inside of organizations trying to bring obstacles to the surface, or sit with a corporate coaching client, after they have told me their desired outcome and what they are striving toward in their shift, I ask these simple questions: "Are you at this desired outcome right now? If not, why not?" One way to posit this question is as follows: "Do you go home every night confident you are on the way to reaching your desired outcome?" If they answer "no" (as most people respond), I ask, "What stands in the way that you'd like to remove if you could?" Once these questions are asked, the floodgates usually open and people share their individual obstacles, team obstacles, and company obstacles, or a combination of all three.

Many organizations find it productive to have groups from different areas in a room at once having this discussion. It's the classic case where sales blames back office operations, the back office blames sales, client services blames the manufacturing and quality control, and vice versa. When they are all in a room together noting obstacles to overall firm goals, most often there is an "Ah-hah!" experience on the part of everyone participating that they actually have shared obstacles and they have a chance to combine resources and thought leadership and solve the obstacles overall. The blame game is a much loved one inside of organizations, but it prevents teams from solving the actual problems. Pulling the teams together and asking them to solve a problem together helps to remove a blame mentality.

Write It Down!

If you are a leader of a group, or a team working together on this, here's how to proceed: Start with a blank piece of paper. Look back to your desired outcome, the thing that matters most to you. What has prevented you individually or your team, or may in the future prevent you, from reaching this goal? Why haven't you reached this goal already? What stands in your way?

We all have something that prevents us from doing what we want to do with or within a business. It can be anything—not enough time, not enough money, lack of knowledge, lack of connections, etc. For example, when management tells everyone to do more with less but doesn't help to define exactly what the priorities are, and how to do this (which is more and more common in most organizations), they are putting an obstacle in front of everyone without looking at the cause and effect.

When you capture your obstacles, don't worry at the outset about organizing them—just write them all down. But be sure to be specific. An obstacle like "not enough time" could really be "we're spending too much time discussing plans, not implementing them" or "we can't develop a website because we don't have the time." Putting general overall obstacles is often not productive. You want to drill down and define what this obstacle is really about.

The degree to which you can make the obstacles specific is the degree to which you will have additional options to solve them. As you list your obstacles, keep asking yourself "What do I mean by this?" and "What is the real issue behind this obstacle?" One way to check yourself on this is to consider whether someone else reading your list could figure out what you mean by what you've written. In other words, don't give it short shrift—be sure you have thoroughly identified and thought through what you mean and why it is an obstacle to you.

Take the time now to brainstorm and identify obstacles that have held you back, or that you fear may hold you back on the way to reaching your desired outcome. Don't judge anything; just bring them all to the surface. Go ahead and write them down now using the "Identify Obstacles" worksheet on the next page.

I've noticed over the years, as I've gone through this process with people and company teams, that many times the same underlying

Worksheet 2: Identify Obstacles

As I look at the desired outcome, why aren't we there today? What is preventing us from reaching this goal?

If I am an individual or team member within a company, what obstacles do I face? What obstacles does my team face?

List the obstacles here:

obstacle repeats itself with a bit of a different twist. For example, if a team isn't meeting their goals and we are trying to uncover what's in their way, the list may include such things as "Need more direction about what we are supposed to do," "We aren't sure whether we are being successful month-to-month; need more feedback," "Difficult marketing environment," "Management doesn't seem to know what we are up against," "No tools to sell against our competition," "Not enough people to reach our goals," etc. As they list obstacles and we turn page after page to post on the wall, a theme may begin to emerge. For example, from the above list, if generated by a team like this, it might become apparent that an underlying obstacle is lack of understanding about what their management wants from them. The three following obstacles are really the same thing with a different twist: "Need more direction about what we are supposed to do," "We aren't sure whether we are being successful month-to-month," and "We need more feedback." In short and as a summary, the obstacle here is a lack of communication and information.

Find the Themes

Review your own list of obstacles and see whether or not you have themes emerging from the obstacles you have identified. Are there things that appear on your list over and over but with a slightly different twist? See if you can recognize these and consolidate them before you start to group them. You will find as you brainstorm that you do have some repetitive ideas.

The next step is to review your list and organize the obstacles into the three categories: (1) those you can control, (2) those you can't control but can influence, and (3) those that are out of your control. You may need to force yourself out of your comfort zone on this one, as it will come down to how much control you feel you can exercise over different areas of your life. Recently, in one of the college classes

I teach, we were going through this exercise. I have two classes back to back, and in both we were talking about the obstacles that might prevent a student from reaching the desired outcome of achieving all A's. One of the obstacles was "Having classes I don't enjoy and find difficult to pay attention in." My first class was adamant that this was within the student's control—to prove this, they suggested for example that one could develop a different attitude, one could try and find something good about the course, one could keep focused on their overall goal, etc. On the other hand, my afternoon class was adamant that this particular obstacle was completely out of their control. "If you hate the class, you hate the class" was their general agreement. All of which is to say that the categorization process is a personal one and your ultimate groupings may differ from those of other people. However, the example in my college classes notwithstanding, there is generally a common agreement about the groupings and over the years I haven't found that too many arguments erupt in the process of organizing. Typically the truly "out of one's control" list is pretty short—most obstacles are either movable or can be influenced in some way.

Take, for instance, the story of Polymer Technology Systems, or PTS. As a company, PTS managed to overcome obstacles presented by globalization. Not only did they overcome the obstacles presented, but they quadrupled sales of their cholesterol-checking device in only three years, exporting to 70 countries around the globe. Operating out of Indianapolis, Indiana, their sales reached $15 million in 2006 by establishing cheaper communications models and good international contacts, by tapping government resources, and by creating alliances with larger companies.

The key reason globalization presented an obstacle, however, was that PTS was a relatively small company. With globalization making it possible for customers to access the offerings of companies all over the world, PTS was at risk of losing out to larger firms with better resources and more money to invest in infrastructure and the maintenance of operations. Was being a smaller company out of their control? Yes, but was having difficulty making it possible for global customers to access them within their control or at least within their influence? Yes. Once they could categorize and really understand what was fixable and what was not, they could make decisions that would address the obstacles. In their case, PTS took the initiative to form key alliances, most notably with Boots, the largest pharmacy chain in the UK in 2004, but also with local distributors of their products.

PTS also took the initiative to do the research to pursue the best relationships, the most profitable situations, and the best resources to support the globalization of their business. A program offered by the Export-Import Bank of the United States provided important components for the company to manage its exports, guaranteeing bank loans to help them manage cash flow, helping them overcome the issue of having to wait, on average, between 90 to 120 days for payments and the problem that most banks do not lend on international receivables.

So being a small company didn't hold them back. They identified where the problems would come in, and then created plans and strategies to put themselves in a strong position to compete.

The company has also undertaken a lot of research to find the most affordable options for communication, taking advantage of the Internet and other forms of modern technology. They use the Internet for market intelligence and to identify potential distributors, and e-mail and mobile phones for easier and cheaper business communications.

The key to overcoming the obstacles was first to identify them — to understand what they are, how they are categorized — and then to consider ways to remove or overcome them. In this case, PTS, in order to overcome their obstacles and continue to grow, had to establish innovative, out-of-the-box thinking.

If you brainstormed a laundry list of obstacles and grouped them so you were not overly repetitive, it's time to review your list now. Again, first consolidate any obstacles that seem to go together, and next consider where each obstacle fits. Use the categorization worksheet on page 58 as a guide to help with this process.

Taking the second step in the process by highlighting your obstacles and categorizing them can often be the primary catalyst you need to make change. If I identify the obstacles that stand in my way and I know which I can control and which I can influence, I can methodically and specifically start to put my plan in place.

At a minimum, it mentally frees me from the time and frustration I have been spending on obstacles out of my control, and it allows me to clearly see the things I can control or influence.

Let's say my goal is to bring in a new Chief Operating Officer to work side by side with me and to help make my company more efficient. One big obstacle might be that I am the primary stakeholder and decision maker in the company, and I am unsure of what new perspective I want to bring to the business; my colleagues always tell me how comfortable they are with the current arrangements, and so I am hesitant to put a new person in place. Perhaps as I list my obstacles, most of them revolve around this issue although I notice them in different ways—my own inertia in putting together a job description, my view that there is a lack of talent in the job market today, a lack of clarity we have as a firm about what this role should actually do for the company, etc.

Once I can see these obstacles clearly, instead of feeling threatened by them or overwhelmed by how much I have to address, my plan for change may actually emerge from looking at the obstacles

Worksheet 3: Categorize Obstacles

Obstacles within my control:

Obstacles within my or the team's sphere of influence:

Obstacles completely out of control:

in black and white and then putting them into the categories. Once I know what I am up against and have a framework in which to view the obstacles, I can incorporate steps that will address each one of them as I make my plans to create the shift. In this example I might realize that part of my process will be to open communication with my staff, or involve them in the process of constructing the job description. I might brainstorm with them whether it's actually a Chief Operating Officer we need, or some other role within the firm. If I can see the obstacles clearly, then categorize them and not just ignore them, I can make plans that address them.

It's actually the not knowing that holds us back — we resist or we think we can't do something, or we make excuses why it isn't possible. When we can clarify them in black and white, organize them, and then look at each one, it actually allows us to be much more productive toward solving them.

© Randy Glasbergen.
www.glasbergen.com

"If you know how to turn obstacles into opportunity, why do I have to move my toys off the stairway?"

Obstacles can, in some cases, present opportunities to us — information we find we don't have, ways we have done things in the past that haven't worked, factors in our lives we weren't thinking about beforehand, etc. All of these can come to light and give us the opportunity to work with them in an effective way. Many a leader or team has had what I call the "Ah-hah" experience when they've taken the time to catalog the obstacles. Clarity around what's actually holding them back emerges, and past frustration can turn into productive next steps.

Rather than feeling like you've made a list of why you can't, or complaints about what stops you, you may actually find this stage of the process very freeing. Any time we can see things more clearly and have a better understanding of what we are facing, we have more opportunity to put a plan and process in place that's workable! Again, it is a language shift, but if you simply change the word "obstacles" to "opportunities" for those issues that are within your control or within your ability to influence, it opens up channels for creative thinking and changes.

Obstacles are oftentimes movable objects and just represent a speed bump in our path rather than a complete blockage. Creating a plan without identifying and taking into account obstacles is like diving off a boat in shallow water. Simply seeing the obstacle allows you to move to safety. Moving forward without taking the time to identify and categorize your obstacles means you will either find yourself redoing something, or completely stuck.

Following Todd Galant

Once Todd knew his desired outcome, we asked him and his team to capture the obstacles standing in the way of both filling this role with the right person, and keeping the person with the firm. They listed things like:

1. *no clear job description,*
2. *lack of talented candidates coming through the pipeline,*
3. *inefficient hiring process,*
4. *not enough time to devote to finding the right person,*
5. *new employees experience "baptism by fire" when they arrive, and*
6. *no clear reporting structures.*

This list of obstacles contained almost all "can control" or "can influence" items, and it opened the firm's eyes to a recognition that the problem wasn't just in finding the right person, but also in fixing some of the infrastructure around the role. These obstacles were unidentified before the process began, but they gave Todd and his team something to work on once identified.

Another example of the power of identifying the obstacles...

Chris, a business owner, brought my firm in to provide sales training to his customer service team. They needed to cross-sell more effectively, and he was frustrated by the lack of success they were having. We defined the desired outcome and then did an obstacles session before the training began. Chris was very worried it would turn into "an unproductive complaint session where they just list all the reasons why they can't make the sales goals." Instead, the group uncovered and organized a number of very real obstacles, including an outdated customer relationship management system, conflicting goals between the different teams, a lack of knowledge, need for more training on products, and more.

Chris was surprised to learn just how many movable obstacles the team was facing. He was also surprised at how invested his team was in identifying the blockages and in finding solutions to move around them. He and his team put their attention to getting the obstacles out of the way, and by the end of the fiscal year the team had exceeded their goal by 140%. As another side benefit, Chris found his team bringing many new ideas and offering solutions to problems they were facing instead of the complaining he had heard in the past. The process actually shifted the entire culture within his firm.

"Dealing with people is probably the biggest problem you face, especially if you are in business. Yes, and that is also true if you are a housewife, architect or engineer."

—Dale Carnegie

CHAPTER 3

Identify the Human Factor

As a certified behavioral analyst and someone with an avid interest in what makes people tick, I've come to see over the years that many of the problems in business environments that prevent the success the firm desires are actually rooted in something to do with the human factor — either within the individuals or within the relationships with other team members. In fact, as I travel around talking about how people can build relationships and communicate more effectively, the one common obstacle I find everywhere is having "difficult people" standing in our way. I've never done a workshop or a talk where I didn't have 100% of the people present raise their hands when asked if they have difficult people in their lives, preventing them from achieving their happiness in life. It is a universal experience, and yet probably the most overlooked and under-valued part of any change effort. Ultimately the human factor will impact whether change comes easily or whether it is something we fight all the way.

What's the human factor? It's the combination of internal and external human issues. Internal factors are the ones within you, the ones that lurk inside of you. They are also the factors that impact your organization from within—you and your coworkers, employers, or employees. External factors are the other people around you who affect you in some way or those factors that affect your company from the outside—often called stakeholders because they have, or exert, some sort of influence over the outcome of the stated goals.

Internal Human Factors

Internal factors are anything you have accumulated throughout your life or through the life of your company, depending on whether you are focusing on yourself and relatively personal goals, or an organization and its goals. Internal factors either get in your way or help you to succeed. Let's face it—sometimes the human factor falls under the category we previously talked about as "obstacles." Part of what stands in our way often resides in our human element or the people around us. These can be things like a deeply rooted fear of failure, or the message that you received from a negative person in your life, someone who tells you, "You can't do that—you'll never succeed."

Internal factors can also be things like a tendency toward procrastination or an unrealistic view of your own abilities. Within an organization, they can also include issues like poor communication or conflicting objectives. The firm culture is also an internal factor, and employees "feel" a certain way about the company based upon their experience of the culture that has arisen largely from human factors, such as the style of the leaders, or the values espoused by management. A human factor internally could play out where the boss is a yeller, someone who likes to pick on people and call them out for mistakes. People in the firm learn to feel afraid to speak up, and this creates a negative human factor component for the firm. On the positive side of the ledger, the internal human factor could be your resiliency or your organization's resilience, a force of will that allows you to plow through situations that someone else may find frightening or worrisome. Maybe the leaders of the firm have a high level of confidence in their own abilities and those of their staff, so this plays out in a "we can get it done together" kind of culture.

The leader of any given department or business strongly influences the internal human factor for their area of responsibility. Do they engage in gossip? Are people free to speak up about things? Is the leader comfortable taking risks? Are they able to ask for help or support where it's needed? These aspects of how the leader operates and what they put forth as important will impact the perception that employees and staff have about the human factor in their firm.

While the human factor often represents an obstacle, we look at it separately because the people component and how people behave has so much to do with the experience employees, team members, etc. have on any given project or in any given firm.

What Holds YOU Back?

As you read this, you may see that on a personal level, as you examine areas you wish to shift but haven't been able to, you will probably find that some internal factor is holding you back. It could be an internal human factor, i.e., something within you, or it could be an internal factor within your organization, part of your organization's cultural makeup. It depends whether you're focusing on an objective that focuses on you or one that primarily involves your organization.

Common internal human factors I hear about from corporate executives I deal with generally are things like an inability to effectively manage time, a propensity for procrastination, inordinate amounts of unreleased stress or frustration, an inability to control emotions, fear of failure or fear of success, and a lack of clarity about what will really bring about happiness. Of course, many of these issues are pertinent to the workplace, and employers and managers have some stake in how well their employees are able to deal with these human factors. Obviously, the better a person can manage time, avoid procrastination, deal with inordinate amounts of stress, and control their emotions and fears, the happier they are. Then they are more likely to be effective and happy in their professional as well as their personal lives. It's why organizations put emphasis on wellness programs, and giving employees "perks." If I feel good about coming to work, I'm often a much more productive contributor overall.

In a recent meeting I was having with a corporate coaching client, he was telling me about his resistance to a new plan the management was putting in place. He expressed a very negative reaction to the request made by his manager. I asked if he wanted to improve his performance in his manager's eyes and be considered for a promotion or bonus? He answered, "Of course!" We then discussed how his negative resistance was preventing him from thinking about how to do what his manager asked. Instead, he was wasting precious time being frustrated about the request and wasting his personal energy. The boss wasn't going to change her mind, so his internal human factor response was only limiting his ability to be successful in her eyes.

If someone tells me they have been trying to reach a long-sought-after goal, and time and time again, they find they are unable to make the shift, I ask them about their resistance. We'll talk about this in more detail later, but from a human factor perspective, resistance is a common reaction within organizations. People may not outwardly say "I won't do this" or "I can't do this," but they will put up walls of resistance in order to stay where they are and resist change. If a change is not happening, sometimes the individual or the manager needs to ask what internal human factor is preventing them from being able to free up the energy to shift.

To catalogue the impact of our human factor in our quest to get to our new desired state, we have to be willing to be self-reflective and honest. It's often easy, and all too common, for us to point our finger at the people who are hampering our progress or not helping us to achieve something. When we look inside, though, we sometimes have a hard time being honest about how *we* might help or hamper our own efforts. This isn't meant to be an exercise in bashing yourself about all you've done wrong or to work through your deeply rooted fears; it's merely an exercise in acknowledging their existence and ensuring that your ultimate plan includes a way to deal with the human impact.

Identify and record human factor issues that you know exist. When you reach the disciplined action stage, you will likely find even more that you may not have been aware of. Even though we may desire a change, we are often the saboteurs preventing ourselves from getting to the very change we desire. If we don't acknowledge this, bring it to light, and work with it, it will remain there — hampering our ability to make our desired shift. Before you compile the internal human factors list, it's important to be clear on what is and isn't an internal human factor.

Too often people believe that an internal human factor is actually an external human factor. What I mean by this is that we have the human factor that lies inside of us — our own thoughts, feelings, education, behavioral style, communication approach, values, expertise, and emotions, for example. Then there are the external human factors, which are all of the people in our lives who may impact our decision to shift in one way or another.

In many cases we'd rather point the finger elsewhere and say that someone or something else is holding us back — if not for a negative person or circumstance, we'd be where we want to be. But imagine for a moment there is no one else in your life and you are faced with the opportunity to make your shift right now — this very minute. That sales objective, that team cohesiveness is just sitting there for the taking. What is keeping just you alone from grabbing hold of it with all of your might? Is it truly someone outside of you that is preventing you from moving forward, or is there something you could choose to do differently?

Watch What You Say — to Yourself and Others

This is akin to recognizing the Achilles heels in your internal human factor. Instead of denying the negative messages you have heard in your life, wishing they weren't a part of you, recognize that these aspects exist. Acknowledge that they get in your way so that you won't ignore them. If you have tended to do something that hasn't benefited you in the past, instead of doing it again and again, acknowledge it. Don't just ruminate over it, but make it part of your planning process to address it along with the other steps you will need to take.

Once you recognize the negative messages you've heard in your life, once you've analyzed them, they will generally cease to be immovable obstacles and you can plan a way to deal with them in your process toward shifting. The problem actually persists if we pretend these internal human factors don't exist or we try and hide them from ourselves. The process of identifying them and acknowledging their existence can oftentimes make them more objective to us — this way, they become a part of our planning process that we need to consider instead of some kind of failing that we have. Even when your goal is to make a meaningful shift in the direction of your business, being able to confront your internal belief system (and possibly being able to help others do the same) means that you are in a good position to overcome what might very well be some of the biggest obstacles on your road to change. Particularly if you are in a management position, you should be ready and willing to challenge your internal belief systems, making sure that, when addressing issues with your organization, you look to yourself first rather than, possibly, blaming your employees.

To create a plan that will work for you, first identify those times when you blame others when the problem may really be about you. Don't be afraid of these times, though—these experiences make up part of who you are and you can work with them. They have to come into the light so you can raise your awareness and take them into account as you make your shift.

One coaching client I had (I'll call him "Harry") kept saying that he would be more effective in his role and take on more risk if only his boss wasn't so angry and verbally abusive. When we explored both internal and external human factors, he admitted that it was really he who deep down did not want to put himself "out there" and make a fool of himself. In our discussions about why this boss affected him so much, Harry disclosed the fact that he had grown up with an angry father he was afraid of. As a child he had lived lurking in the shadows so as not to face his father's wrath, and the feelings aroused in him by dealing with this boss were awakened and took him back to his childhood. Somehow he had transferred these feelings as a little boy with his dad to his boss, and he found himself engaging in similar "hiding" behaviors. It wasn't so much the angry boss as it was a sort of flashback to feelings he had not shed from his boyhood. While our discussions were not of a psychological nature, simply exploring the reaction Harry was having to his boss allowed him to consider why these reactions took root within him.

As we talked further, Harry also acknowledged that he was not a risk taker in life in general, and he feared his colleagues and his wife would ridicule him if he went after a position or another level only to fail. While he had spent a great deal of time talking about the boss, talking about his wife, and talking about how his colleagues would react (perceived external human factors), in reality he had to admit that his biggest holdback was really himself—his own baggage from his past and his current-day concerns about how he might look to the people who mattered to him if he failed. Now I'm not a social worker or a psychologist, but in this case Harry was aware of the deep-seated issues he still had with his dad and he was able to admit his fears around failing. When he expressed to me one day, "I know I shouldn't say this, but I feel like it's my father yelling at me again," I knew that he realized the connection but maybe was uncomfortable talking about it in detail. Some of us don't have the benefit of such self-awareness or the ability to spend hours with a shrink, but we often do recognize certain connections with people or behaviors we have that trace back to something we experienced in our lives.

Once Harry realized and identified what was going on, he was able to create a plan that honored this concern but gave him ways to work effectively with his boss—as his boss and not his pseudo-father. He went after the position and obtained it—with the full support of his wife and his colleagues. He also learned ways to confront his boss professionally. Harry will admit that each day is a work in process, but at least he recognizes the issue for what it is—an internal human factor for him—and he can continue to deal with it as such. He had to push himself out of his comfort zone to reach his goals, but he found a sense of relief in giving up the blame he had carried around and the feeling that he was at the mercy of those around him.

By contrast, you can also use the positive aspects of your human factor to your advantage and recognize where you can leverage them in your shifting process. Internal human factors are not always negative; they also include those things that can serve you as you work the process to shift. The process asks you to look at and uncover strengths and attributes you may not be focusing on, or that you may not keep front and center as you shift in new directions. Do you have a core competency that gives you confidence in working toward your goal? Are you a compassionate leader who connects well with others and can use this skill to motivate your staff? Do you have an ability to reframe bad situations in a more positive light to make them easier to deal with? There are many skills that we possess that we don't take the time to catalogue and consider as we endeavor to make our shift. If you are a person who has a hard time uncovering those things you do well, or where you specifically could contribute in a change effort, ask others who know you well to help you with this step in the process.

To illustrate the importance of the human factor, we worked with a firm that was in a very specialized market and very successful in their field. They were an entrepreneurial management team and a very learned and educated set of leaders. They were in a fast-growth mode and were hiring people into many different positions at a very rapid pace. They found, after a few months, that making decisions within the firm was becoming increasingly difficult. In one case, a major client was left without an upgrade that had been committed to because the firm hadn't made a final decision on what they needed to do in order to respond. When we looked at the human factor, the management team admitted they had always valued consensus decision-making. As a team of three, they'd never made a decision that they hadn't all agreed upon. As the firm grew so rapidly, they'd tried to extend this consensus approach to all team members. At 16 people, reaching a decision had become almost impossible in any reasonable amount of time. The leaders hadn't realized they were doing this — it was a default decision, because they had always valued hearing everyone's input. Once they realized that a previously beneficial approach had now become a detriment to the firm, they could look at it more critically. They decided to create a clear decision-making process that differed for each area of the company and by the decision that had to be made. They kept some issues for consensus by all team members, but many issues were determined by management alone.

This human factor had evolved without their awareness of it, and once it was identified, they were able to come up with a working process that made sense for the firm — but allowed them to keep their integrity about what mattered to each of them as individuals. The human factor can be specific to one individual, it can be a cultural experience such as had evolved from this team of three, or it can reflect how team members end up working together.

As a leader within a firm, or a manager of a team, you want to pay close attention to your internal human factors. It's often the case that a leader won't want to reflect on how his or her behavior may be impacting the team or their employees. The leader might feel like they can say, "Just do it!" and get agreement and adoption by employees. But sometimes the employees are resisting and reacting to the style of the person in charge. Honest self-reflection is not easy for most people, but if you are a leader who really wants to gain loyalty and support from your team, looking at how your approach impacts others is a critical step.

Begin to make a list of your internal human factors. Again, it requires some honesty and self-reflection. Especially if you are the leader of your firm, or in a position to influence change, remember that it isn't about just finding what holds you back. It's also about identifying factors that will help your team to make the shift. Recognizing the positive things that we have to offer can also help us to create a more effective and actionable plan. In our example with the consensus approach by the management team, reaching consensus could be considered as a positive, but extending it past the point of being productive turned it into a negative. You will want to catalogue things about you, your culture, and your teams that are both positive and negative. The negatives become part of the obstacles, and the positives become leverage points as you make plans for your shift.

Use the questions below to list the internal human factors that come to mind as you think about shifting toward your desired outcome:

- What internal human factors (emotions/past experiences/ personal beliefs) do I identify as obstacles to my effective participation in an organizational setting?
- Conversely, what internal human factors might help me make a shift within my organization?
- What human factors are positive outcomes we recognize in our firm culture?
- What human factors negatively impact how our culture operates?
- What internal factors can be identified as obstacles to the effective progression of our organization toward new goals?
- What internal factors might help the organization make a shift?

Review the lists you have made here. Has your human factor list led you to any new obstacles to add to your original obstacles list? If so, go back and add them now.

To effectively put the S.H.I.F.T. Model™ into action within any team or organization, it is ultimately all about leveraging the energy of the people and the firm overall; getting clarity of focus and direction, and using feelings, information, and practical tools to shift confidently in a new direction, whether in your personal life or within an organizational setting. The human impact is very often the element within a firm that derails the process—teams that can't work together, bosses and employees who can't connect, staff members who feel slighted and that the firm just doesn't care about them. All of these human aspects, if not addressed, steal time and money from the company. Without a dedicated process, such as I outline in the S.H.I.F.T. Model™, that asks team members to examine their contribution and personal experiences, the biggest part of any change effort—the people—gets overlooked. This step allows you to identify the positives and the negatives and make them part of your solution.

If You Know It, You Can Fix It!

I was teaching my Leadership class at Suffolk University, where we teach the S.H.I.F.T. Model™, and I asked the students to raise their hands if they found procrastination to be a problem for them. About 75% of the students raised their hands. A little later I asked them how many felt confident they would procrastinate and wait until one to two days before the paper was due to start to working on it. The same 75% raised their hands again. This is a great example of the human factor. If I know I am a procrastinator and can admit to this "failing" of mine, why would I set out to do things exactly the same way I always do them? Could it mean that I like the stress, or I don't really want to make a shift in a new direction to make my life easier and perhaps make myself more productive and successful? Is this something I need to work on to make my shift?

If you do want to make your shift, use the opportunity to identify your human factors. After all, if getting to a new and better place is your goal, why not recognize how something may have held you back and resolve to take different steps, or alternatively recognize that something is a strength that can benefit you as you make your shift?

External Human Factors

The external human factors are all of those people who have a say in something you are doing or attempting. When we are talking about personal goals, personal shifts, these external human factors could be anyone in your life: family members, colleagues, employees. When we're talking about an organization, a business, the external human factors are everyone outside of your organization that has some level of involvement in it, such as customers, vendors, or investors.

Let's generally refer to external human factors as "stakeholders" because they have a stake in how your shift will eventually turn out. They are the people who in some way could influence, support, or derail some of your change efforts.

There are a few different stakeholder models used in businesses. The most commonly used stakeholder model puts people who have a stake in the change on two scales: power and interest.

A low interest, low power person or group might be a factor, but not a person or group that requires a lot of your time and energy.

By contrast, your significant other or key coworker could be defined as a high interest, high power stakeholder as you plan to take on a new business project. They could be a stakeholder with a great deal of control over your destiny and your ability to shift effectively. They may exhibit a high interest in what you are doing and how well it is working, and also a high power in their ability to provide financial and emotional support—or withhold it from you when you most need it.

There are also low power, high interest stakeholders. Your mother,

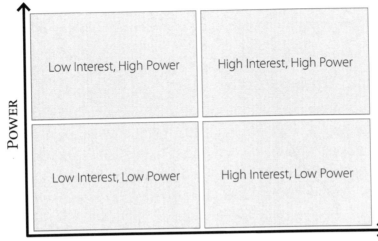

for example, may not be able to help you with a new business plan but she might still be involved because she wants to hear every single thing you are doing. Although she cannot help you materially, she provides a high interest shoulder for you to lean on. High interest, low power people can sometimes be a good sounding board as you make your plans. They have a significant interest so they care enough to be focused on what you are doing, but they aren't really in a position to control or influence anything for you.

Conversely a high power, low interest person could be your landlord. They may have no interest in learning about what you are doing and why, but may exercise their power by placing limitations on what you can do with your business if it is run out of your apartment. This is a category we often overlook, because they don't represent a clearly interested party and we don't notice them in our planning process. However, when we are ready to shift, their high power stake could kick in and they could be in a position to either help us significantly or stop us from taking our next steps.

Stakeholders are all around us, and if you ignore their presence at the planning stage, whether planning for a business or personal shift, they will somehow come into the picture as you make your shift. If they represent an obstacle, you should plan around them, and if they are a positive resource you should leverage their power and interest to help make your shift.

Obviously, and depending on the shift you're trying to make, stakeholders may be few or many. If your shift is to become more involved in a local charity by writing press releases and doing public relations work for them, your stakeholders might be limited to your spouse (more time away from the family), the charity you are working with (or at least the contact person there), and the local media with whom you will interact to get publicity. But if your shift involves getting to a new position within your existing company, there may be many stakeholders in the way — your current boss, your future boss, your colleagues, your significant other, your good friend in your current department, the HR representative, etc.

The human factor applies to each of us as individuals as we try and forge our way through change, and it also applies when companies are seeking to reach a desired outcome. Many a time I have worked with a senior executive seeking change and they have reported resistance within their staff. Most times, the resistance stems from the fact that the new plan wasn't taking into account the different stakeholders and their stake in the change. Rather than identifying these in advance and making them part of the planning process, the firm just imagined that "everyone will get on board eventually." The trouble is, as anyone who has worked in a situation like this knows, "eventually" rarely arrives! The idea for shifting might have been a necessary and well-thought-out idea, but the shift doesn't happen because stakeholder resistance and the best ways to engage those stakeholders weren't considered in the planning process. As we've seen with many aspects of the S.H.I.F.T.™ approach, if we know there are stakeholders, we can create plans that take them into account and use them productively in the process of shifting.

Recognize the Resistance

When we think about stakeholder resistance, let's consider that resistance can also occur with desires we may have on a personal level, too. It's very easy, when the management of a company appears to be making significant changes to its operations, for employees to become nervous about their own future in the company. If the implementation of any of these changes depends in part on the employees, there may be resistance to change driven by fear — fear that they (your employees) might be replaced or find their job no longer available. I was leading a significant change effort at a company I worked for in a very senior capacity. We were creating a vision and excited about where we were going. Everyone on the senior management team felt confident about the new direction and was moving forward in a positive vein. Because I had an open door policy, I started to have people who had been with the organization for quite some time stop in more and more often and ask me about how the change would impact them. What would their new role be? I started to realize, admittedly a little too slowly, that the changes we in management were so excited about were causing significant worry and distress in our staff members. The "not knowing" was becoming so distracting that team members couldn't focus on their day-to-day efforts. We neglected to take into account our most important stakeholders — our employees. The time and energy that had been lost, by the time we realized this, was significant. Ultimately we put a communication plan in place and ensured that employees were involved in knowing why and what we were planning. If we'd done this at the outset it would have saved me personally a great deal of time, and would have led to an overall more productive process.

Worksheet 4: Identify Stakeholders

People around me who have a stake in the outcome of what I am planning (or the business is planning):

What is their interest or stake?

As you think about your stakeholders, look again at your desired outcome and the shift you are hoping to make. Think about all of the people who may have some sort of stake in the process—if not now, then at some future point. Brainstorm, using Worksheet 4 on page 81, to identify them and what kind of stake they may hold. Don't worry initially about categorizing; just get all the names and ideas down so you can see who you consider to be your stakeholders. Remember that the stakeholders in your life are different depending on the shift that needs to happen. It's not a generic list of people who impact your life in some way; it's a list specific to the people who affect your shift process and your goal.

Next, look at this list and put the stakeholders into the traditional interest/power categories, using the worksheet on the next page as a guide. This, again, is the most common grid used to categorize your stakeholders. It does so according to who has either low or high interest, and who has either low or high power.

As with all of the steps, this one will require you to capture what you know now. But it's an evolution, and as you begin to develop alternatives (in the next step) you may find there are other obstacles or other human factors that you didn't identify the first time around. The process can't be entirely linear—not many things in life work that way—so it requires you to think as you go through, so that ultimately your plans have considered all of the necessary components for your success.

All of the stakeholders may be important in some way, but the ones that appear in the top right-hand corner (High Interest, High Power) are the people you want to manage most closely in your change process, and you may not even recognize them at first. As an illustration, in a class I taught to graduate students called "Dealing with Difficult People," one of the women was working with a not-for-profit which wanted to do more outreach in the local community.

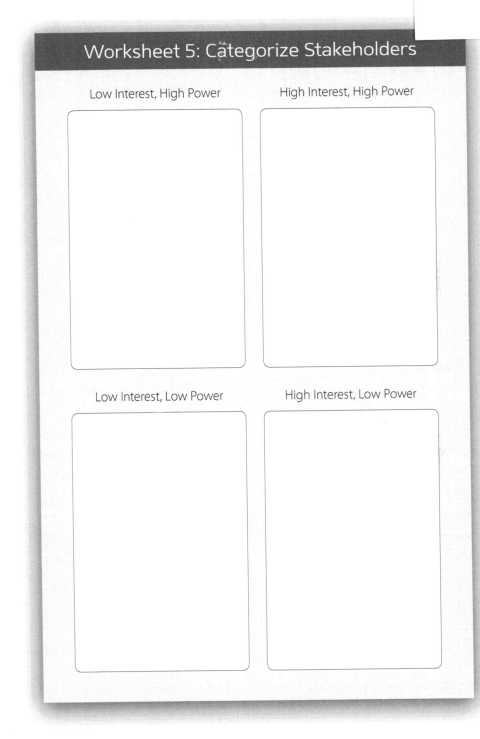

Worksheet 5: Categorize Stakeholders

Low Interest, High Power

High Interest, High Power

Low Interest, Low Power

High Interest, Low Power

The desired outcome was established, the plans were made and the objectives set. The obstacles were identified and categorized and the stakeholders were identified. The plan began to take shape, but there was one outspoken group of residents in the area who had been overlooked. They were not overtly wealthy or powerful, but within the neighborhood they were well known and had a great deal of clout—a different kind of high power status.

As it turned out, they had a great deal of interest in what was being planned, too. They were able to completely derail the plans because they hadn't been consulted or asked for their support. Fortunately, subsequent meetings took place and they became allies, and ultimately became one of the main reasons the project was successful. But this story is a great example of how good plans can go awry when you attempt change without considering and leveraging the stakeholder interest. The not-for-profit never even thought about this group, and yet they turned out to hold the key to ultimate success. It is better to take everyone into account initially as you make your list of potential interested parties, even if you end up leaving them out of your change process, than to miss someone or some group that holds an important stake. Clearly it is not wise to assume you have support, or assume that you can ignore someone because they don't seem to care or to have power. Anywhere our lives touch another person's, for right or wrong, that person may have a stake in what we're doing and might have the ability to help—or hamper—our effort toward change.

Following Todd Galant

When Todd looked at the human factor within his firm and his situation, he recognized both internal and external factors. He admitted that internally, he was predisposed to believe that a new employee should "just figure it out." He knew that he was easy to anger, and was feeling frustrated with the lack of progress that each person who came into this role had shown in their first few weeks. While he didn't enjoy admitting it, he saw that he was quick to judge a new person if they didn't measure up in his opinion. In addition, when he looked at the stakeholders and considered the external human factors, he found there was confusion among other staff members as to what this role really meant, so they harbored resentment toward new people coming into the firm. Because of this resentment, the existing staff didn't do anything to help a new person in the role, and each person hired found themselves floundering. During a discussion about human factors, we looked at Todd's behavioral and communication style ("just do it and don't bother me with the details!") and his staff members' resistance to a new person and new role. Both of these were worked into the obstacles and planning process, and were addressed in the new plans to design the role and find the right candidate.

"In my case, if one out of five opportunities is interesting enough to work on, maybe one in five of those ends up being worth doing. That might be a function of risk. That might be a function of price. There are all the variables. But you have to be constantly sorting and choosing and prioritizing."
—Sam Zell

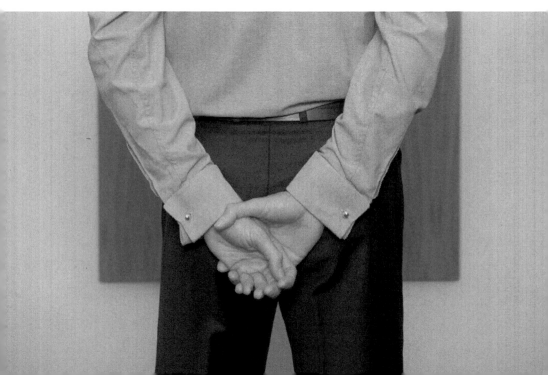

CHAPTER 4

Find Your Alternatives

W hen a business manager has applied the solutions presented so far to manage change, they have all they need to start actually planning how to achieve key goals. The desired objective should be clear, the obstacles highlighted and categorized, and the human factors captured. It is time for the key business personnel to brainstorm alternatives to help reach the desired outcome, work through obstacles, and address any human factor issues. Oftentimes when I am speaking to large groups or corporate teams trying to change course, I'll ask how often in the past they thought they had a good solution to a goal they wanted to achieve, only to find out it really wasn't a solution at all. This is a universal experience, sometimes called "the best-laid plans of mice and men," where we think a direction or solution works only to run into the same obstacles again.

It's an occurrence I see all too often with my business and individual coaching clients. The tendency is to hear the problem or the desired outcome, and then leap directly to a solution. Many times in the leadership class I teach, once the not-for-profit organization has presented their challenges to the class, the students feel—just by hearing what the firm is trying to achieve—that they know how to get there. Unfortunately the initial solution is not always right. In some cases it's not only not the right solution, it actually makes our lives more difficult. This applies to the small decisions we need to make in our businesses and of course can extend to many different aspects—the person we hired in as our successor to the firm, the job we covet and then find to be a poor fit, or the business trip we take that ended up in food poisoning because we didn't plan appropriately and take the necessary precautions!

Defining Criteria

We'll move on to looking at the alternatives your team or company may have to make the shift you desire, but first you, as leader or with the team, will want to identify your decision-making criteria. This is another thing I find that most people and the businesses they support do at an unconscious level, but don't really capture in black and white on a conscious level so they can work with it. Establishing criteria is simply capturing those aspects that are important to you—or in some cases non-negotiable. Having a set of criteria gives you some guidelines and a lens through which to view what options might be best for your specific firm and your specific situation.

To illustrate how we use criteria in decision-making, I often use this personal example with my Leadership class: If you were hoping to move to a new location, what criteria might you take into account before you made a decision where to live? The students might respond with things like "being in a safe location, being close to public transportation, being somewhere warm, the cost factor, having more than one bedroom so I can have a roommate, being in the city, being close to my work or school." It's not hard for them to make a list of the things one might consider when making a move.

But, when I go around and ask them to prioritize their criteria, I will obviously get different answers. One person might be adamant that the backyard has a pool, and another person might say they would never own a home with a pool! So the criteria list should be prioritized so you can be reminded of what matters to you and what factors need to be considered. I've seen many firms, for example, create a plan for a marketing initiative but not set criteria around how they want to measure it, or what costs they want to limit it to, or what aspect of the plan will be most important to them.

In one example of how developing criteria can provide a guiding force, I had a coaching client who was miserably unhappy in her job. She identified those things that were dragging her down and created positive outcomes for her criteria list. She then prioritized the most to least important. Her list included things like: A boss who wants to collaborate, a location no more than 10 miles from my home, flexible working hours, a position that allows me to use the skills I have developed in this industry, and a collegial working environment. Based upon her past experiences she knew what she didn't want, and translated this into her criteria and objectives. She then set out to find a new position, keeping this criteria list clearly in front of her. She ended up with a job that met all of her important criteria and was also more money than she was making. She considered this to be an added bonus, because she hadn't even had this on her original criteria list. The criteria gave her a lens through which she could view different job options and consider them. Having prioritized criteria gives us some personal, or firm-related, guiding principles about what matters in our decision-making process.

Some people might feel like this is unnecessary time spent to consider the list, prioritize, and write it down. They might say, "I know what's important to me." And certainly the fact that a firm or team may not take the time to write down criteria in the planning process doesn't mean they don't have them. But it's worth taking the time to actually catalog them in such a way that we can see them and work with them more efficiently. This process is grounded in bringing elements of a change process to light, in order to give a firm the opportunity to work with them in a clearer and more proactive manner. Criteria might often be assumed within a company, but when management gets in a room to agree on them and "cement" them, they find they have many differences of opinion that haven't been discussed.

Criteria for many firms, depending on the decision to be made, can often include things like time, money, physical constraints, and employee engagement or interest, but depending on the desired outcome you have, there could be many other factors that you want to identify. If you set the criteria and agree upon them within the team, it makes the decision-making process much easier. If we all agree, for example, that the number one criterion in determining which new product to bring to market is that it has to be one that can be released within the next 18 months, we will then remove from the list any of the products slated out past this time. In many team situations arguments rage over the best idea, or the best way to proceed, because the criteria aren't really clear. Getting agreement and clarity at the outset will provide the entire team a roadmap for further decision-making.

I was facilitating a meeting with a colleague of mine, and the group consisted of board members, management, and employees from this company. They were trying to make decisions about what initiatives to focus on over the next 12-24 months. The management team was a bit concerned about what it would be like to have board members and employees interacting in one meeting. In order to keep the conversation focused on the goal, we started out by listing the criteria for their decision-making and then creating the priority list. The exercise of creating the list was a bonding experience in and of itself. The board learned about some of the employee concerns and objectives, and vice versa. They were able to develop a core set of criteria they could all agree on, and then each initiative was considered against this list. By the end of the full day's discussion, they had a working plan with the top five initiatives they had agreed upon and steps to take to implement them.

As you work on your list of criteria, think about why different criteria are important to your team, or business. Why is the item important? What kind of priority does that item represent for you or your business? Ultimately you want to prioritize the list and determine the non-negotiable aspects. As you put a plan in place, you may have to choose something that meets only some of your criteria, so you'll want to be aware of the most critical criteria for you.

List the criteria of the desired outcome you are trying to reach — what kinds of things you want to take into account as you move toward your desired outcome. What will be the important decision-making factors that will help you decide between different alternatives?

After you list your criteria, put them in priority order. Your business may not be able to meet every priority so you want to be clear, in advance, about what matters most. List and prioritize your criteria using the "Define Criteria" worksheet on the next page.

Preparing to Brainstorm

Now that you have created a list of what matters, you can begin the brainstorming process. Be sure you have the time and opportunity to focus on this before you start to think about your ideas.

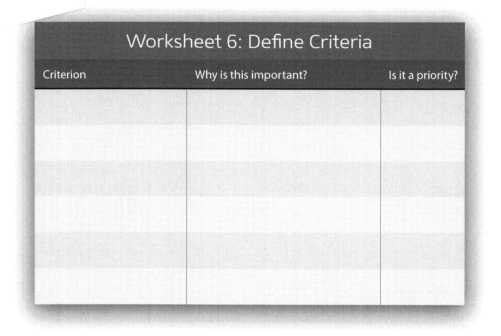

Worksheet 6: Define Criteria		
Criterion	Why is this important?	Is it a priority?

You want to have all of the pieces to the S.H.I.F.T. Model™ to work with before you begin. Keep your desired outcome clearly in front of you before you start. Once your business has taken the time to identify what the desired outcome looks like, either post this in front of the room to remind everyone of your definition of success or circulate it in writing to all team members. At this stage, you can also spend time giving a bit more detail about (1) what this outcome means to your team or your business, (2) what exactly success looks like when you get there, and (3) how your business or team will be different once you reach the goal. The important thing is to have your desired outcome written down and documented, and then circulated to all decision-makers or contributors so you can focus on it with clarity.

Let's say you have chosen to enhance the corporate culture within your organization and want to be more sociable and involved, encouraging your team to, with appropriate regularity, engage in fun activities as a team. In addition to the written goals, you could "act as if." This is a technique that requires seeing the outcome you want for your team and business before it happens. The team might talk about the organization as if this is in place—what's happening, how do they recognize that this cultural shift has taken place, what's different now? The discussion surrounds not what they currently have in place that they don't want, but rather what it looks like in detail when they get what they do want. It's a discussion that places people in the frame of mind of experiencing the positive outcome.

In addition, acting as if—if you are the firm leader, for example—could mean painting the picture and visualizing the positive outcome of the change for your team. It could mean celebrating the progress that's being made and focusing your attention on what's working well as the change unfolds. Alternatively, if you are an employee or team member working within an organization, and your

**"We're devoting two years to develop a
five year plan to revise our three year plan
for the implementation of our ten year plan."**

desired outcome is simply for your team to work together more effectively and with more satisfaction to reach departmental goals, try to visualize things like communicating openly, enjoying working together, reaching your financial objectives, getting accolades from your superiors, and being happy about coming to work. This paints a clear picture that you can keep in front of you while you brainstorm. It orients your mind and your discussion toward what you do want, instead of focusing on what you don't.

And while it was very important to capture your criteria and prioritize them as you brainstorm your options, you may find that you need to alter your criteria a bit to give you more latitude. You could want to do this because you might not feel as good about your final outcome if it doesn't meet all of your important criteria. You are always left with the option of keeping your criteria in place and finding solutions that fit by simply disregarding anything that doesn't meet all of your criteria, or by finding a solution that meets most of your criteria but leaves you a bit of wiggle room. The main thing is to be conscious of what you are doing. We often sacrifice something through reactive decision-making, and then we regret having done it when we realize what we have given up in the process.

Some Brainstorming Techniques

There are many types of brainstorming techniques to help you get around obstacles and reach your desired outcome. If you have a team environment and there are a few people trying to figure out what to do, let's look at some of the options you have for coming up with ideas:

Round-robin—this approach allows each person individually the time to think about what they believe the best solution is. A facilitator is elected within the group, and the facilitator goes around to each person and has them give at least one solution that they think is workable. The process should not stop at any one person, but should allow everyone to suggest at least one idea before any of the ideas are reviewed and discussed for viability. The recorder in the group captures these ideas so they can be reviewed later. No idea is dismissed out of hand at the time, but rather everyone gets a chance to propose something and they all go on a list for the group to review together at the end of the round-robin. Sometimes it is useful to go around more than once to solicit multiple ideas. All ideas are recorded and posted for the team to consider against the criteria. In some cases, this approach leads to a couple of different ideas being blended together to come up with an overall solution.

The important aspect of a round-robin is that everyone gets to contribute before any ideas are discussed in detail. This can help to avoid the common occurrence in a group where one person is more forceful and proactive about sharing, and someone else who is less forceful might get overlooked. Instead of looking at ideas one by one, ideas from every group member get listed and discussed at once.

Visual mapping — this is where the group uses Post-it® notes to write ideas down without talking and then posts them on a wall, or in the middle of the group on a table. Team members each write a number of ideas on the sticky notes and then put them all on a wall or table to view. Once the notes are all displayed, they can be moved around and combined as the group discusses the best routes to their desired outcome. A facilitator can help here by standing up and asking the group which notes belong together and which can be moved to the side.

The nice thing about this approach is that no one knows which member of the group wrote on which piece of paper, so it feels more anonymous. This can sometimes lead to better overall outcomes, because people tend to look at the ideas more objectively. Even if I favor my idea, I may see something else that could combine to create an even better outcome. In fact, in many cases the solution is a combination of many different individual ideas.

Mind mapping—this process begins with a piece of paper with the desired outcome in the middle. The group then draws lines from the middle with different ideas, which then branch out to other ideas. For example, if the group needs to increase its customer retention rate, the middle part would say "Increase customer retention," and some of the offshoots may include "Talk to our existing customers," "Ascertain client satisfaction," "Survey clients," etc., and from each one of these, other ideas would grow. "Survey clients" might have branches that say "Call our top 15 customers," or "Contact a survey firm," or "Set up a Survey Monkey account," etc. The point is that one idea can lead to another until a way to move forward starts to develop. The end result looks a bit like a spiderweb, with different lines coming off and then going in another direction. Each branch of the mind map will lead to an idea that represents a limb off the branch. As the group makes the connections and connects the lines on the mind-map, different ideas emerge. Instead of taking the traditional linear approach to decision-making, this approach allows the team to go in a number of different directions before a final direction is determined. For an example of mind mapping or to download a free version to help your team use it effectively, please visit www.biggerplate.com.

List making—this approach involves each person in the group using a different-colored pen. A paper is circulated and each person uses his or her pen to write an idea down as the paper is passed around. There is no talking, and the ideas aren't discussed until there are at least two options for each color of pen. The facilitator can then read the list out loud and the group can discuss which idea they want to further explore.

These are examples of good ways to brainstorm in a team situation. As an individual, the process of brainstorming is a bit different. Using brainstorming techniques — and applying them with little deviation — can allow for a greater universe of ideas and often better ideas than normal group problem-solving. However, many studies have been done that actually show when individuals brainstorm on their own, they often generate more ideas and sometimes even better ideas than groups of people who brainstorm together. So, as a firm leader you may want to spend some time generating ideas on your own. Even in a team setting, you could ask each person individually before a meeting to generate a list of ideas they bring to the meeting they are prepared to discuss.

When you begin to brainstorm as an individual contributor, don't immediately default to seeking advice from people you know. Carefully review what you've done so far with the S.H.I.F.T. Model™. Review your obstacles in their respective categories. Next, review the human factors: your internal feelings, concerns, and emotions, or the stakeholders you've identified, or both. Go through these lists and watch what your mind starts to do in terms of possible solutions. Sometimes ideas start to come together as you review your lists. We often seek outside counsel but if the other person, no matter how learned they may be, does not have access to all of the information generated to date using this model, they may jump to a conclusion that doesn't address the root of the problem.

If nothing pops up when you look over your obstacles, take out a piece of paper or open a Word doc on your computer and write "What can I/we do?" at the top of the sheet. Then list all of the things that come to your mind. Don't qualify or judge any of your ideas at first, just get everything you consider on paper. You will ultimately have to consider each option against your criteria list, and in light of your identified obstacles and human factors, so you don't need to qualify ideas as you list them. Just allow your mind to give you any option that might exist — you have a clearly outlined process for considering them that will guide you.

Beware of Naysayers

Be sure when your team reaches this stage of your shifting process that you don't share your ideas or ask for feedback on what you are trying to accomplish from other groups or teams within the organization whom you might expect won't be fully supportive of your endeavors and solutions. On every team, and within every organization, there are people who want to tell you why something won't work. That isn't the case, thankfully, with everyone, but you really have to guard your plans as you continue to flesh them out. Hopefully when you identified your stakeholders and your internal human factors (perhaps you're the one who throws cold water on your own plans and ideas at times), you recognized this dynamic. Sometimes we are our own worst enemy (internal human factor) and sometimes it's the stakeholders around us (external human factor). What's critical is to know where the negativity may exist and avoid it until you are ready to open your idea up to criticism and debate.

If the brainstorming process proves difficult for you or your team, you can capture your potential alternatives in writing in initial sessions and then let the list sit for a day or two. As you or your team turns away from the process and focuses on something else, you'll find that ideas will start to germinate and take hold. For example, it can be helpful to brainstorm at one meeting, type up notes and circulate them, and then schedule a next meeting to create a plan once everyone has had time to digest all the proposals. Use the "Identify

Worksheet 7: Identify Solutions

Potential Solution	Against the Desired Outcome	Control/Influence Obstacles	Human Factor	Criterion	Ranking (1-5)

Solutions" worksheet on page 99 to list your ideas. When you come back to your list in a day or two, go through it and consider each possible solution against:

- **Your desired outcome.** How do your ideas bring you closer to the outcome you desire?
- **Your obstacle list.** As you look at what you can control and what you can influence, do your solutions allow you to overcome the obstacles that might be in the way?
- **Your human factor.** Do your plans address any internal issues? Which of your stakeholders will support you in it and how?
- **Your criteria list.** Do the solutions meet what's important to you?

You might want to create four columns next to each solution so you can go through and consider each one against the four categories.

What Can You Do?

As you review the ideas you have brainstormed against the four categories, you should start to see which ideas seem most workable and which do not.

It is key to remember at this stage that you aren't seeking a single perfect answer. You are seeking the best answer that will give your firm the greatest possibility of reaching the desired outcome that's been agreed upon. Have the team help to identify which idea you will commit to, and then clearly move forward without second-guessing whether you should have selected one of the others.

In one case, a small firm we were working with felt they had tried everything to grow their business. To each idea we raised, they would respond with "We tried that and it didn't work." They were feeling stuck and in need of a catalyst or plan to move them forward. They went through the entire S.H.I.F.T. Model™ and arrived at the stage of finding alternatives. They felt they had done it all before, but agreed to try a brainstorming session and use the model to look at their issues. What emerged was very exciting to the team members. Ideas they hadn't thought of before came to the surface, and one of the newer, younger team members had one of the best ideas which eventually became the basis for their final plans. It was another example of how simply having a process can allow for ideas that hadn't previously been explored to emerge. This team went into the process thinking it was an exercise in futility and yet the outcome was an energized, excited team focused on implementing a new program for growth.

Following Todd Galant

Once Todd and his team got to the stage of Finding Alternatives, they had many ideas already in place about what they needed to do. These criteria included making a decision that was valued because it was workable and would solve their problem, rather than simply because the decision was quick. The alternatives they found included things like not having a new position at all, but rather blending the position into current positions; creating a job description that clearly outlined the requirements; creating a new interviewing structure involving members of the team; hiring a recruiter to take care of the whole process, and more. Todd found that given some of the obstacles they'd identified, even in the brainstorming session he wanted to be very specific. If an idea didn't have an opportunity to address the obstacles, he didn't want to focus on it. The team still ended up with several workable options for finding the right person for the role in their firm.

Todd's team then reviewed each alternative against their criteria and considered the pros and cons. They were surprised at how many different ways they could solve the problem, once they took into account the obstacles and human factors and focused on the desired outcome.

"Greatness is not a function of circumstance. Greatness, it turns out, is largely a matter of conscious choice, and discipline."
—*Jim Collins*

CHAPTER 5

Take Disciplined Action

If you have been successful in brainstorming a few possible ideas and you have been able to identify a solution that appears to be the best fit for your circumstances, it's time to create your plan. Of course, as you've seen throughout the book each stage has its associated difficulties, and creating the plan is no different. In business and in personal situations it is common to hear someone announce a grand idea. They've written down their objective clearly, they can paint a picture of the idea, they can tell you all the components of the idea, and they can even engage you with their excitement and confidence, but what they can't tell you is how they are going to get from here to there, step by step, in detail. This is the most difficult part of the process in most situations, because the devil is in the details.

A senior business leader may tell me about a plan he or she has for improving the business and finding new revenue sources: "We're going to provide education and materials to our clients on topic X, and in doing so it will help them to refer us to their friends and family members." Okay. Sounds reasonable in theory. But who is going to provide them with this information, what does the information look like, what is the follow-up plan, how are they going to assure that the client actually will refer people to them, who is going to get compensated for overseeing this, for implementing it, and so on? At this point the senior executive will often look at me quizzically and simply reply, "They'll figure it out." The problem is that people often don't "figure it out" and that's why bosses and businesses, spouses and significant others, children and parents get frustrated. Expecting people to know exactly what is necessary doesn't always work, because oftentimes they don't even have a clear view of the big picture, never mind each discrete step of the process.

As I was writing this book I had occasion to meet with one of the very senior people that I provided coaching to at a large client firm. She was sharing with me one of the new initiatives the management has asked them to implement. I asked her about how she was going to roll out the request to her group. What steps did each of her team members need to take to implement the new ideas? What had she set for timeframes and milestones? After answering a few of my questions, she looked at me and said, "Management always has great ideas of what they need us to do but they never help us develop a plan to actually do them!"

This illustrates the common occurrence within organizations — set an objective, come up with some good ideas to drive toward that objective, but neglect to break it down into discrete and manageable pieces so that employees know what, when, and who will do each step.

But How Will You DO It?

In my leadership class, when the students try to solve a problem that a business has brought to them, they will usually come up with great ideas and solutions as soon as they hear the problem the business faces. They will very excitedly share their solution to the challenge that has been raised. That is, until I ask them how exactly they plan to implement their solution. They will often look like the proverbial deer in the headlights at that point and ask, "You mean we actually have to be the ones who take the steps necessary to put this in place?"

That's what taking disciplined action is all about. It's fun to create ideas and brainstorm solutions and pontificate about what we are going to do someday, but the only people who actually make the change happen are the ones who can clearly identify what next steps they will take to get them closer to their goal. I'm continually amazed by how many businesses and people want to get somewhere but don't have a written plan as to how they are going to do it. This doesn't mean creating a business plan and writing a novel about all of your ideas; it just means identifying your shift, taking into account all of the aspects you need to think about, and then determining what step-by-step actions you will take to get you from here to there. All plans, no matter how detailed, are not foolproof. Life definitely intervenes, and sometimes we have to make a mid-course correction or go down another road to get to our desired outcome. But just because there may be a need for a detour in your trip doesn't mean you don't bother with running the MapQuest report in the first place to figure out how to get to your desired destination!

Moving to the End Goal

How does the process unfold from here? You've reviewed all of the alternatives you could come up with against your criteria, and you've decided which one you want to implement and the corresponding path you will take. Let's look at an example scenario we've already considered in this book: Say you want to set up a new website for your business, to give your company a more compelling online presence. You already have a website but you want something that's more up to date, more dynamic, and suited to helping you create a new distribution channel online — selling to customers directly via your site.

Assuming you've done your market analysis and have determined fundamentally that this is a good idea for your firm, your disciplined action plan might look something like this:

1. Identify a couple of people within your organization who are able to assist you with the website planning and development, or set out to recruit a qualified person from outside the organization to assist.
2. Determine exactly what you want this new website to do.
3. Review the current website with your team and take account of changes you want to make (the gap analysis).
4. Schedule time to discuss your plans with the senior stakeholders within your company so that everyone is aware of the proposed development and has an opportunity to offer suggestions on how the site should be developed.
5. Identify appropriate website design software, shopping cart systems, etc., to support your site design requirements.
6. Establish a budget and cost constraints for each aspect of building the site.
7. Schedule a time during the work week to allow your site development team to work on the various components — site planning and development, etc.
8. Set a clear timeframe for the change and schedule a time each week (or whatever is convenient) to review progress.
9. Create the site with appropriate website design software and

review the site for technical issues and quality.

10. Allow your stakeholders to review (and hopefully approve) the site design.

11. Publish the site.

While some of the steps in the process may seem self-explanatory and even basic, writing it all down in detail gives you a much greater percentage possibility of doing each of the steps. It's all too common to overlook something, and have very good intentions, but find we didn't think enough about whatever it was to include it in our plans.

Think about the common to-do list that most executives and others use in their day-to-day work. It's typically a list at a high level outlining what that person needs to accomplish. In many cases, though, the things on the list could easily be broken down into more specific and detailed steps. Doing this allows that executive to engage others in the implementation process. Something on the list like "Prepare presentation for our internal Town Meeting session next Wed." can be broken down into components: Determine what to focus on, get a count of who will be there, develop PowerPoint® presentation and handouts, establish whom to call upon to ask for their input during the meeting, etc. This small example shows that something that appears to be one line and one item actually has a number of components associated with it. Figuring out what each component is allows the person to delegate or take pieces of the overall process at a time to put them onto a calendar and plan more effectively.

At a recent client event, I was presenting a planning concept along with a colleague from my client firm. The audience was learning steps to take to implement a new marketing program within their firms. The process was clear and presented in a step-by-step fashion. At the end of the $3\frac{1}{2}$-hour event, one of the participants said, "This is all great but I'm so busy. When do I find the time to do this?" It's a great example of knowing we need to make a shift in our businesses but not finding a way to actually do it. The implementation stage requires you to identify each component, and then assign responsibilities and time lines. When you can break something down into discrete steps, you are able to find ways to take each step. Not having a plan in place is what derails most good ideas.

Let's look at a real world example that I observed at a client firm. They had a management team of seven people who had similar jobs and were able to cover for one another. This group of seven met with the desired outcome of working together more effectively so each person could work a four-day workweek. They went through the steps in the model, and after brainstorming the idea they finally selected was to put together a schedule of rotation so that all shifts were covered but no one worked more than the four days.

The disciplined action might include the following:

1. Make a list of the activities that need to be accomplished by each person so we know that everyone is covering everything they need to during the shift.
2. Set up a schedule with the dates and times for each shift.
3. Put each person's name next to each date.
4. Circulate the list so that everyone can read it and approve their date/time and name.
5. Put a communication list together with each person's name, email, phone number, etc.
6. Circulate this list so that each member of the team can get in touch with every other person in case of a missed shift or an emergency.
7. Provide reports to management at the end of each week showing all that has been accomplished during each shift so that management feels supportive of the four-day approach.

8. Meet once per month via conference call or in person (decide on a standing time) to review what has been done and make any adjustments.

Each step in the process was broken down to its finest level of detail so that nothing was left to the vicissitudes of assumption. Even the contact list was discussed: Were they to provide their information to one person to consolidate and then circulate to others? Were they to send it via email? Was it to be posted in a master list? The final plan was very specific.

Assuming that others know what we know and will do what we would do in the same situation is a dangerous flaw in many plans. Each of our styles is different; our values are different; our education, background, and knowledge levels are different, so we can't assume that because one person knows what to do in detail at a given step, everyone else does too. To ensure effectiveness in meeting the desired outcome, the plan must be granular and specific steps must be outlined and assigned.

Break it Down!

Part of the detail is the "who" for each step. We can say "Make a list," but we also have to identify who will make the list. Who will be responsible for creating it and then circulating it? A name must be assigned to each step, along with a deadline and any potential budgetary considerations.

For example, in the earlier scenario of developing a website, you were asked to capture the cost of the site's development and identify a team to work on the site design. Anything that might derail a process, like an unanticipated expense or not knowing who is responsible, must be identified in advance.

This is a good discipline to develop in general. I've lost count of the number of times I have been in a meeting, or participated in a conference call, and all of the people present have agreed on some sort of follow-up. The next step, however, is never crystallized. Agreeing on a next step is only half the process — figuring out who, what, when, how much, etc., is the other half. Without that second half of the step, time rolls on and our "meant to do that" creeps in. Because we haven't taken the time to capture, record, and lay it out, we simply don't get to it. It's just too easy to move on with the other demands of life. Many frustrating meetings could have been avoided if the people running the meeting had implemented this one step at the end: Before the meeting breaks, record who, how, what, and when, and then make sure that everyone is clear on their tasks. I'm reminded of the importance of this when my students ask, "How many pages? Double or single spaced? What size and font do you like?" and so on. Their questions remind me how much detail we really need to offer so that we can receive the outcome we are looking for in its entirety as we want it, and when we want it.

To help in this process, I have created a simple implementation plan (shown on the facing page) that I use with my corporate clients and individuals to outline their disciplined action.

This plan allows you to list each step in the process and think about who, when, how much, and so on. I find this planning process helpful even in my day-to-day to-do lists.

Have you ever read a book about getting clutter out of your life? This seems to be a chronic problem, and there are an abundance of books on the subject. Pick up any one of them and the author will tell you not to think about cleaning the whole house at once, but rather about starting in one corner at a time. There are two reasons for this: first, because we feel a sense of accomplishment if we take on something and complete it; and second, because it reduces the job so it seems more doable. Rather than getting all of the drawers

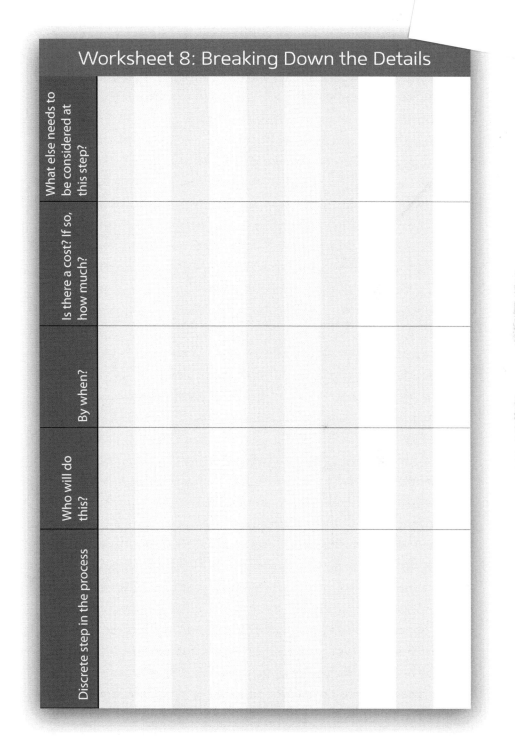

Worksheet 8: Breaking Down the Details

Discrete step in the process	Who will do this?	By when?	Is there a cost? If so, how much?	What else needs to be considered at this step?

pulled out in every room and then being unable to complete the process, taking one small corner and finishing it in the allocated time actually gets something done.

So to recap, the process of breaking down the plan into specific, discrete steps is where you finally take your disciplined action. Your plan should outline your target dates and who will help you and what you need to do. Keep this plan visible, even if it means carrying it around with you. You may want to transfer each of the steps to an Outlook® or Google™ calendar or some other task list you rely on. Each day that you need to complete something, you should have the step clearly defined and incorporated into your calendar so that it isn't an "if," but rather a "when." Don't leave anything to chance at this stage of the process. You've worked hard on each step of shifting to this point, and this is where you need to commit to breaking down your steps and finding ways to work through each part of your daily, weekly, or monthly plan. You know what you need to do, so set deadlines and assign steps in the process to others wherever you can. Use the "Breaking Down the Details" worksheet on page 113 to do that now.

Having a method to capture what you need to do, and to keep yourself on track, is absolutely imperative to your success with this process. Once you have your plan, review it and be sure you have a detailed time line associated with what you need to do. Do that right now, and before you do anything else, take those dates and write them in your calendar. That binds you to a written commitment and confirms the time and date of what you will do and how you will do it.

Determine other methods that will help your organization keep on track. For many people, writing on 3×5 cards works well. For others, having someone to whom they are directly accountable works better. The latter is particularly appropriate when you are working within an organization. You can quite easily identify someone to monitor your progress toward key objectives in your shift. Even more specifically, that person can oversee your progress toward the completion of specific activities.

Some people find using a tickler system very helpful, such as the "Getting Things Done" (GTD®) approach by David Allen, where everything you commit to goes into your GTD® system with appropriate dates and commitments.

Color-coded folders are yet another approach. I once worked with an organizer who showed me that buying a label maker was the best investment I could make! I have color-coded folders for different projects (clients, books, marketing, financial information), and I can create a separate folder for each specific project. For example, this S.H.I.F.T. book has its own folder and in it I keep a list of when and what I need to do, so I can refer back to it at any point.

There are many, many systems and approaches. Becoming very good at time management can be useful, and in my experience those who are good at managing their time always have some sort of system they use to keep the team on track.

So, make your commitment. Create your plan. Find the way to keep yourself on track and make the shift your business really needs happen!

Congratulations! *If you have come this far in the book, you have created your plan for shifting. In my work with people in their personal lives and in businesses, there are many other factors that I see contributing to one's overall level of success and contentedness. In the second part of this book, I want to share some ideas to consider for an overall increase in effectiveness in many different business settings.*

Todd's Desired Outcome

Todd designed a clear job description and laid out for his team exactly where the role fit within the current organization and how it would support and interact with other roles. He involved team members in the hiring process, and together they developed a list of criteria and questions to ask each candidate. Todd even had one staff member do extensive background screening on candidates to ensure they exhibited behavioral styles that were a fit for his firm. Before a hire was made, the team designed an intake process that was specific and clear, and he put another staff member in charge of integrating the new person. The next hire that was made was a great fit for the firm, to work with Todd and to collaborate with his team. The rest of the staff had become so involved in the process that they actually felt invested in seeing the new person succeed, and they worked very hard to help bring this about.

PART II

Tips and Tools for Greater Effectiveness in Business

"It's not what you've got, it's what you use that makes a difference."
—Zig Ziglar

A s I've worked with senior executives and people at all levels within an organization, I've identified a few key concepts and strategies that everyone can benefit from if they are involved in a business, no matter what their status or where they are trying to get to, no matter what type of business.

In fact, whether you're trying to implement or simply participate in a strategic shift within a given organization, or whether you're just looking to build or be part of a stronger team, knowing something about formal business plan development, internal branding or corporate culture, presentation techniques, and stress management can really help you to set yourself and your team of colleagues, co-workers, or employees on the same page.

Part II of this book holds many keys from programs, coaching work, training sessions, and one-to-one work that I've done over the years, addressing these key areas. I've taken the best ideas about these concepts and skills, and I've put them in this book so you have an idea of some of the strategies you can use yourself and bring to the work place to ultimately improve overall efficiency and enhance the quality of the work environment. These strategies for relaxation and focus also provide suggestions for making change more effectively.

As you try out some of the ideas here, don't lose sight of your overall desire to shift. These ideas and improvements can aid you in the process, but you will still want to follow the S.H.I.F.T. Model™ for long-lasting and significant success. The best way to take advantage of the information in these chapters, in fact, is to find a way to incorporate them into your S.H.I.F.T. Model™. As you will soon realize (if you haven't already), it is not at all difficult to do this. First, to apply the S.H.I.F.T. Model™ effectively, you certainly need a clear plan. You also, at some point, need to make everyone else in your organization, both internal and external stakeholders, aware of what you are proposing. This is precisely what business plans are intended to do, sometimes along with marketing and strategic plans. Indeed, the majority of business advisors out there (including those who have written a ton of books on business development and planning) are not wrong to stress the importance of having a well-written and cohesive business plan to share with everyone in your organization and even those outside of it—most obviously, of course, potential investors. In chapter seven, we will explore some of the elements that go into an effective business plan and what you need to know to develop effective marketing and strategic plans to go along with it.

In chapter eight, we will discuss a more conceptual but no less important strategy for business development known as internal branding. If you think about branding, what a brand represents, you can see that it generally serves as a particular look. A brand defines a company; it suggests not only who the company is trying to market and sell to but also what it is that they value. For instance, GEICO, with their funny-looking British lizard, is clearly out to attract the more no-nonsense types, those who want to get a deal, who feel that they are often in a position to "get" the joke, to call their bluff. Allstate, another insurance company, presents an altogether more sober and somber face. They appear to be reaching out to an older audience and one that is not so much out for the best deal based on cost. Rather, Allstate's primary market is probably older and more interested in a deal that reflects best coverage. The point is, though, that these two companies make a specific presentation to the outside world. Internally, too, they will make a similar presentation of their values, their missions, and their goals.

When an organization is looking to make a shift, a key change, it is vital that everyone in the organization is on board, unified in feeling that they are part of a team. More than that, it is crucial that they feel themselves to be valued team players. That said, the overwhelming majority of companies have very little idea how to brand from the inside out, how to back up their external branding with a clear program to develop a corporate culture consistent with the external one. This is where internal branding comes in and why it is important, if you want your shift to be a success, that you have knowledge of internal branding strategies to apply to your organization.

In chapter nine, we take a slightly different view—examining the importance of communication techniques. After all, when you are trying to implement a change, it's highly likely you will have to actually "sell" it to some of your key business participants. There's only so much you can do on paper, too. With an organizational shift, the creation of a new business, the leadership ought to be inspiring. If you can be confident in your presentation, in the way you communicate orally, particularly to a larger audience, the more inspirational you will be. Also, you may well find that you have your stakeholders in a much better position to help you bring about the desired shift. If they are inspired by your presentation, if you do communicate effectively, it's likely that you will also foster much clearer lines back and forth, allowing for that all-important exchange of ideas and, in more practical terms, even the effective sharing of responsibility.

The last chapter in this section addresses the issue of stress management, the importance of which is based on both the professional and personal components of achieving organizational change. As we will discuss in this chapter, stress is, to some extent, a natural product of just about everything we do in life. There are different kinds of stress. There's physical stress when you undertake just about any activity. It may be very minimal; we may not notice it at all. But it still exists. In some cases, if you ignore stress, it builds up. Sometimes it simply overwhelms from the start, preventing any positive progress at all. For instance, an angry and abusive boss, when they use a negative approach to get their employees to take affirmative action, is very likely to get nowhere at all. They're unlikely to make any progress, particularly if their anger is something that their employees are very used to. Stress management techniques, however, can be beneficial to both reducing stress in a specific instance (stress brought on by a boss's anger in a particular situation) and also in a more general context, reducing it in the long run (helping the boss to manage his own stress levels and thus become less angry and aggressive toward coworkers and employees).

Managing personal stress effectively can also help individuals move forward toward higher degrees of effectiveness and efficiency in their work environment. The techniques outlined in chapter ten, in fact, should be very useful in helping you to hone your own S.H.I.F.T. Model™, allowing you to reduce stress as you implement the model and hopefully improving overall efficiency and effectiveness in the long run.

To whatever degree you apply the various ideas and strategies in this section, however, remember that your success is something that you have to define. Even when you are implementing change for an organization, consider the impact this effort has on your personal relationships and on the other areas of your life that should, based on your interests, receive prioritization.

"*Successful leaders have the courage to take action while others hesitate.*"
—John C. Maxwell

CHAPTER 6

Developing a Formal Business Plan

You need a business plan to start your own business, but you should also have a formal written business plan when you are making any significant change to your organization. In fact, it's common sense to have a business plan on hand even when there is relatively little on-going change.

Unfortunately, most people don't have a clue where to begin writing their business plan, and this is one of the reasons that many businesses don't have one. Sometimes it is because they haven't really thought enough about their business idea. To an extent, the process of writing a formal business plan, like the goal setting we did earlier in the S.H.I.F.T. process, can help you figure out what you are really trying to do, and what the various components are in the process.

Although each one is different, most business plans have the following components:

Executive Summary—this section describes the basic idea behind the company. For all intents and purposes, this section is the general introduction to the plan. A lot of companies choose to explain the reasons for starting the company in the first place. They may also provide a brief summary of the history of the particular industry the venture is based within.

Mission Statement & Objectives—the Mission Statement should establish the company's values, what they want to bring to the table. Presented as bullet points, the objectives of a company are outlined in a business plan so that it is clear to whoever is reading the plan precisely what the goals of the individual and the team might be and what the company cares about and aspires to.

Market Segment Analysis—this section is basically an in-depth review of prospects and customers, those you intend to target with your business. It allows you to outline by segment, such as doctors or business owners, or by identifying ideal traits of the customers you desire, such as those in a life transition, or those who travel a great deal.

Product/Service Information—explaining the importance of the product or service you're offering is all-important; this section generally includes a review of the product or service with a view to point out why they are different from everything else on the market and why it can be deemed that there is a substantial need. Sometimes it's helpful here to outline the problems your product or service solves.

Marketing Strategies—this section explains how the business will be advertised to various audiences. Most business plans provide a general outline of marketing strategies, which are followed up in a marketing plan.

Sales Strategies—these are crucial to the success of a business, so every business plan includes a section devoted to explaining how sales will be achieved. A number of key questions are generally answered: Who will be responsible for sales? How will prospects be converted to sales? How will sales be recorded and increased if necessary?

Personnel Information—business plans generally include a review of the company structure and planning. An important aspect of this is the company staff, or at least the key job descriptions within the organization. Personnel in positions of authority, whether they are managers or executive assistants, can have an important role to play in the development and ultimate success of a company, so assigned responsibilities and relevant skill sets are generally outlined in this section.

Financial Summary and Projections—although financial projections may be based on guesswork, it is vital to outline a plan of the money that will go into the company, and it is also important to try and determine how much money will come out of it.

It's important to have a business plan so you can clarify who you are, where you want to go, and what's meaningful to your business. But its value, as we'll talk about later with regard to communication, is also that without the written plan you can't communicate to your team and your employees very effectively. In many of the firms I've worked with over the years, from small to large, the employees are confused about what's critical to success. It's very de-motivating when a person is going into a job every day and not exactly sure what their contribution means to the business overall. Having a written plan—especially if you can communicate it widely—tells your team you have a plan and lets them know in many cases how they can play a role.

Business plans can be as detailed and complex as the management wants to make them, or they can be high level and simply lay out where we are now—and where we want to go.

Consider the status of Dell Computers in November of 2010. To move in a direction that was necessary and positive, the company set a clear path for change in a business plan. Their key objectives included increases to revenue, as well as cultural objectives for the company, and individual objectives for products. The company planned to make more acquisitions and boost spending on research and development as a long-term strategy to double the size of the company's data center business to roughly $30 billion in sales—their revenue objective. They also planned to be more "patient," keeping the valuation and development of potential targets from escalating as a result of a bidding war for an important storage maker, 3Par, Inc.

Dell explained its objectives on the basis that roughly 55 percent of the company's revenue came from selling desktop and notebook computers, where margins were seen to be continuing a general trend of shrinking. Using acquisitions and research and development spending, Dell hoped to strengthen its business of selling computer servers, data storage, networking gear, and technology services, generating their target of $30 billion in sales by the end of the fiscal year 2014, rising from $17 billion, which was the current sales level at the end of January, 2011. A secondary goal is to increase research and development spending on those products from a single-digit percentage of sales to 10 percent or more.

If they achieve their targets in 2014, though, it will undoubtedly be due to the fact that Dell was prepared to establish a clear and precise plan for their shift. The shift is well justified, clearly defined, and apparently something that the key players within Dell are well aware of and prepared to support. A business plan is crucial in achieving these ends—justifications for proposed changes, clearly defined goals, and organization-wide understanding and support. And while there are many books out there devoted solely to business plan development, any of which can assist you if you have trouble in the actual writing process, the outline above gives you the basic framework to work with, targeting the key areas of information for your plan so that everyone involved knows what direction they should be headed in.

"A business based on brand is, very simply, a
business primed for success."
—David F. D'Alessandro

CHAPTER 7

Building Your Internal Brand

Every business needs to differentiate itself from the competition, identifying the benefits it offers to customers and how it stands apart from competitors. This, however, is a bare minimum for successfully reaching out to customers. For a business to be able to change and adapt successfully (and just about every business has to go through some significant change in its lifetime), it needs to know what it stands for; everyone involved in the business needs to know what it is, what it's about. When you are planning a shift for your business, applying some basic strategies to enhance your internal branding is likely to be very important to your success.

The four most common problems with the internal branding process at most firms are as follows:

1. Employees don't know there is an internal brand;
2. If they are aware there is one, employees don't understand it;
3. Employees don't care about it or don't understand how it

impacts their day-to-day work; or

4. Employees aren't motivated to deliver on it.

Most experts will tell you that about 70% of people don't enjoy going to work. This statistic suggests that despite the fact that people are the most important assets of organizations, the vast majority of employees don't feel appreciated and they aren't inspired to contribute to the organization they work for.

When employees care about their company, they can provide a kind of litmus test on the effectiveness of different elements of the business, particularly when there is a program for change. Companies invariably have a problem when their employees do not feel that they really know their employers or that they have any kind of connection at all to senior management. In these kinds of situations, which are common, employees within an organization feel disenfranchised in the decision-making processes of the company.

You can't have a successful culture without the hands-on involvement of the CEO and senior management team — and brand cultures, as we shall see, only truly work when leaders feel a responsibility for developing a legacy rather than just short-term financial success.

You may also face a scapegoat problem if relationships within your company are less than sound. Middle managers and line managers tend to be the most intransigent, but it is often the case that they are not getting enough guidance or they are being poorly treated themselves. In many firms, the middle managers serve as the "translators" who take the directives from senior management and then have to figure out how to incorporate the mandates into the daily activities of the staff and of the firm. It's key to engage them so that in their role as implementer of the ideas, they know and understand why they are doing what they are being asked to do.

When your employees are inspired, you'll find that they are indeed your most valuable assets, and one of your most effective marketing tools.

The following four goals can serve as guideposts as you begin to consider your internal branding strategy, and give you objectives for the areas you want to focus on:

1. The need to be able to put your market in context so employees understand who you are targeting and why,
2. The need for your organization to be adaptable and willing to change as necessary,
3. The need to make your employees both committed and engaged to the goals of the company overall, and
4. The need to collect measurable results.

One of the most important factors when implementing an internal branding strategy is commitment from your employees to the external marketing brand image. This type of commitment fosters creative contribution from your employees, which now allows you to tap into targeted knowledge because of the direct interaction your employees have with your clients. In many firms I've seen, the employees actually experience a disconnect between what the firm says to the market externally about what they stand for, and how they behave internally with their staff. There should be consistency in image — the external image is pulled through internally. This dynamic is essential in consumer services companies. The company may show the market how attentive they are, and how willing they are to provide support and information, but then internally they treat the very people charged with serving the clients poorly. Employees who are asked to provide enthusiastic support and attention to customers don't want to feel as though they don't matter at all.

By contrast, a company can pull the positive customer experience through so that employees are excited about walking the talk internally as well as with customers. Take the Ritz Carlton Company as an example. The credo for the company is very specific. It demonstrates what the company values and what the management wants from its employees.

The company credo states: "We are ladies and gentlemen serving ladies and gentlemen." It adds, however, that the company's "ladies and gentlemen" (i.e., the staff) are the most important resource the company has in the service commitment to guests. They are the ones that take the lead in applying the principles of "trust, honesty, respect, integrity, and commitment."

The Ritz-Carlton has distinguished itself among hotels by taking a fresh approach in the industry. The credo clarifies the responsibilities of the upper management and makes clear that their function is to (a) anticipate the wishes and needs of guests, (b) resolve their problems, and (c) undertake genuinely caring conduct toward guests and each other.

Because the company has made it clear what image they want to present to the world and what kind of working environment they want to maintain, the Ritz Carlton stands apart from most other hotel chains based on its commitment to excellence and the care of its guests.

If you choose to review your internal branding approach and consider whether you have an opportunity to strengthen it, the first thing to do is an assessment, along with a definition of your specific goals. If you completed the S.H.I.F.T. Model™ you already have some of this identified. You need to get a sense of what you want others to believe, to feel about your organization, but you also need to look at what you want the people within your organization to know about it, to believe about it, and to do to support it. You also need to think about how much you want your organization's members to invest and in what areas—how much time, how much energy.

There is a great cartoon where the manager of a company is standing up on a table and speaking to his staff where he says, "The beatings will continue until morale improves!" This seems to be a credo in some firms. By contrast, putting a focus on internal branding means you are choosing to be more deliberate in your employees' experiences. You set—and communicate—a culture, a philosophy, and the guiding principles. You then work with your staff to integrate these into the daily activities.

This doesn't always mean trying to completely revamp or recreate culture throughout your firm. Internal branding could involve simply organizing an annual party for your department or taking the time to outline the "credo" of your organization. The process of thinking about what matters and how we want our employees to experience working here gives you a basis for reinforcing the structure and unity of your company. The stronger and more unified it is, the more effectively it will be able to handle change.

You can also take some deliberate, calculated steps to enhance your organization's identity. You can, for instance, establish some rituals for your organization. For example, you could establish that Fridays are casual days or that every month, employees compete in an informal game of some sort, bowling or something similar, building relationships and promoting teamwork. You could organize an "employee of the month" reward system to apply values to your organization internally. In addition, some companies promote family values and good health. They offer daycare services and allow employees to go ahead and personalize their work environments a bit, with family photos. They might offer healthy foods only and provide low-cost or complimentary gym access. None of this is just about the value—the immediate benefit to employees. The strategies are designed with a broader purpose in mind: to build loyalty and enthusiasm to support the company.

What's important is that you are deliberate within your firm about what you want the internal brand to be. Many firms develop a brand by default, what employees think and feel, rather than by deliberate actions that drive experiences in a particular direction. If you aren't getting the enthusiasm or response you think you should from your employees—or if you are finding them resistant to change instead of helping to create it—consider whether there is an opportunity to revisit your internal brand and strengthen it.

"If there is any great secret of success in life, it lies in the ability to put yourself in the other person's place and to see things from his point of view—as well as your own."

—Henry Ford

CHAPTER 8

Presenting With Confidence

S o now that you have an idea of how to develop a formal business plan and an internal brand or corporate culture to unify your organization as it moves through a change, let's think about one of the key strategies for actually promoting the importance of change or a new direction.

In every organization the leaders who can present well — to their teams or to their employees — will be the ones who command the attention they need. When we think of presenting, we often think of a large audience sitting and listening to a motivational speaker. This is one form of presenting, but presenting is also about communicating who we are and "selling" others on our objectives or ideas. Whether in a one-to-one with an employee you want to motivate, or with a $25 million prospect, there are six definitive keys to confident presenting that business people can use to be more effective in each interaction. As a leader you will want to know these keys, but you can also share them with your staff members. Everyone within an organization benefits from gaining the knowledge to present ideas more confidently.

Six Keys to Confident Presenting

1. Have a reason beforehand—know why. Many presentations aren't appropriate for the timing, or for the material presented. And many times someone is asked to present to someone but they really aren't sure why they are presenting or what the desired outcome might be. This happens in particular when a third party or salesperson makes the request, "You need to come and meet with this prospect." It could also be when you get summoned to your boss's office to share an update, or when you are interviewing a strong candidate for hire to your firm. Before any presentation of material, if you are asked to go somewhere and meet with someone, you will want to take a few minutes to document the "why?" What's the desired outcome for this interaction? Why is this presentation of information happening now—why not six months ago, or three weeks from now? What is significant about this timing? What is the purpose of this interaction—what does the listener hope to know, or need to know, as a result? Before you even begin to construct your material, identify the "Why?" and identify the desired outcome. It could be many different things: Inform. Sell. Persuade. Motivate. There are many reasons—what's yours?

2. Connect with your audience—know who. It's a common mistake that anyone presenting an idea will work very hard on their message, and know their presentation inside and out, but they neglect to modify it for the audience. What do you know about the person or people you will present to? What do they hope to get out of this presentation? What do they know—what don't they know? In a one-to-one meeting, you can take your materials and show the person how much you have to share, but let them know their time is valuable, so first off you'd like to ask them some questions to be sure to focus your comments. Most people appreciate when you ask, "What would you most like to get out of this interaction? What's most important to you?" In a board presentation, or multi-decision-maker situation, ask to speak to some of the people who will be there in advance of the meeting. What do they hope to gain? What would make it successful time well spent in their eyes? Before you even begin to present, re-establish what you were told in advance: "These are the six key things I've been asked to focus on in this presentation. Has anything changed? Do we have anything else to add?" The more you know about the person listening, the more you can gear your comments to what matters to them. Consider collecting any data in advance through interviews or an assessment of their needs. If you are presenting to a larger group, even ask them questions about their knowledge level—"How many people feel they are better than a 7 on a scale of 1-10 in knowledge of this subject?" and things like this. At least you get a sense of your audience and what they might know, or be expecting. And remember, "it's all about me" for most of us, so if you can talk from a place of value—to them—you will gain a listener and probably a follower, too.

3. Create flow. In many presentations, the presenter tries to pack a lot of information and data into one continuous flow of information. The result is that the receiver isn't exactly sure what fits where and how to assimilate the information. Any presenter will want to look at their information and "chunk it" into manageable pieces. It's best to stay within the bounds of seven sections (or less) of information. As you look at all of your material, what chunks emerge? Organize the information into these chunks—"I have three key take-aways I want you all to have" or "There are six reasons why I am recommending this course of action for our firm." Chunk so that your listener can follow your line of thinking. You want to think about the following: (a) What's your overall topic or subject—what are you hoping to accomplish and convey? (b) What segments or chunks do you have within the topic? What are the groupings of information you can make? and (c) What's the information within the segments? What specific points do you want to make? You want to create an introduction—no matter whether to one person or a group—and tell them what you will tell them. Give them an overview of the segments you will cover: "I have three key points" and then list the areas you will cover and refer back to that list each time: "In this section about international equity, let me show you our dedicated, selected managers and why we've chosen them." Open and close each section so that the listener knows what information they are being asked to pay attention to.

4. Make it matter—provide context. As an extension of the chunking process, don't leave it up to chance that the listener will understand why this information matters to them. So what that you have improved the quality of your dishwashing liquid—what does that matter to me, the listener? This is where you want to refrain from assuming anything. We often think it's clear why we are saying something, or why someone should care, but with the information overload most people live with every day, we can't possibly wade through what's presented to us and have a clear idea of why it matters and what we need to do about it! Keep asking yourself the "so what?" question. So why does this concern your audience, why does it help them, why might they need to know it? Make it clear! If you can't give context, and clarify the meaning of what you are presenting, consider whether you need the information in there in the first place!

5. Match behavioral style. Particularly in one-to-one meetings, but also in small groups, a presenter of information wants to listen and watch for the other person's preferred style before they engage. Watching someone else's style and then modifying your communication approach is a great way to connect with them. What's style? It's our tone of voice, our pace, the words we use and our body language. If I am, by nature, a slow-talking and thoughtful person but am dealing with someone who is fast-moving and quick to learn, they will get aggravated in many cases by my different approach. If I am a "results-oriented" person who is working with someone who needs time to think, time to process, and time to consider what I've said, that person may be turned away by my brusque approach. In order to communicate with impact and be heard the way we want to be, we need to stay aware of our own style and watch that of others. Excellent presenters will naturally modify in reaction to their audience, but most of us have to work at it! When dealing with a group of people, use different approaches in order to appeal to different types of people. According to the research that has been done on this topic, when we don't adapt our style to that of our audience, we lose a percentage of our effectiveness.

6. Bring closure. This means bringing your audience around to what you started out with as the objective. What did you hope to accomplish from this interaction — sharing of information, need for a decision on some data, the "close" in a sales process? This is where you must remember to come back to what you desire out of the interaction and to ensure that the listener(s) received what they need. Before you leave the meeting, or presentation, if you had a desired outcome, reconfirm it. "As a result of this presentation, I wanted you to understand three things" — then list the three things. "Next step, I'm asking each member of this audience to…" Vote? Give me a business card? Buy my product? Be sure when you end the interaction, whether one-to-one or in a group, that you have confirmed and closed what you hope will happen next as a result of your speaking with them.

Using these keys to confident presenting, in any exchange, will allow you as presenter and the material you are presenting to stand out and have a chance at being effective and meeting your desired goal.

Worksheet 9: Present With Confidence

1. Know why — what is the desired outcome of your presentation?

2. Know who — describe the target audience for your presentation.

3. Create flow — identify the main sections and key points in each.

section topic	section topic	section topic
key points to make	key points to make	key points to make

4. Provide context — why does information in each section matter?

section one	section two	section three

5. Match style.

What is the behavioral style of my audience?

How can I adjust my presentation to match this style?

6. Bring closure — list your presentation's "take-aways" or next steps.

Note: Your presentation may need to have more than three sections. If so, use an additional sheet to capture the required information for steps 3 and 4.

"It makes no sense to worry
about things you have no
control over because there's
nothing you can do about
them, and why worry about
things you do control? The
activity of worrying keeps
you immobilized."
— Wayne Dyer

CHAPTER 9

Managing Stress

S tress comes in many forms. There is so-called "good stress" that motivates us and drives us to reach new heights, and then there is so-called "bad stress" that consumes us and makes us less effective in our day-to-day activities.

For better or worse, most aspects of our life create stress to some degree. In the work place, within an organization, stress management is not only practical but quite important when it comes to the pursuit of goals.

In my experience, any unmanaged and unwanted stress is bad stress. That said, in both your personal life and your professional life, within the organization in which you work, there are several options for diminishing stress, even channeling it. Emotional stress factors are just as painful as physical stress factors, and must be considered and treated gently. As much as possible, it is helpful to try and integrate some of these stress management techniques within your organization, although the right approach to managing stress has much to do with individual behavioral styles. A person who is an energetic, physically active, and fast-moving type will need to dissipate their energy with physical activities—by taking a run, climbing a mountain, cardio-boxing, and the like. Someone who is more laid-back, quiet, and calm will need quiet time or alone time to recharge their batteries.

Just Breathe!

Proper, deliberate, controlled breathing is a great way to reduce stress. One of my clients went to a coaching program for a week and came back very excited. He told me that after almost 50 years, he finally learned how to breathe! And believe it or not, learning how to breathe effectively made a significant difference in his feelings about his work, his family, and his life.

Another important way to alleviate stress is to take breaks throughout the day. It's hard to sit for hours on end, or stand at a machine or in a showroom for hours, without some kind of a break. One of my coaching clients was experiencing an undue amount of stress and was having a hard time sleeping at night. She was so overworked that she found herself being unproductive in many activities. We agreed that she would set the timer on her computer to remind her to take a break every 1.5 hours.

For her this meant actually getting up and taking a walk around the floor on which she worked. I asked her to think about a song in advance that always cheered her up, and as she walked to sing this song in her head. She reported that just when she would be feeling uptight, the reminder would go off and she would force herself to get up and take the walk. When she came back to her desk, inevitably, she had more focus and more energy to go back and deal with whatever had made her stuck.

What are You Worried About?

Do your best to dispense with worry, especially as you move toward your desired goals. When the English author and Anglican priest, William Ralph Inge, wrote about worry and the act of worrying, he said that "...worry is the interest paid on trouble before it comes due." I read about this concept in a book by famed motivational speaker Zig Ziglar many years ago. He advised his readers to make lists of things that worry them so they were out of mind and onto paper, where they can either be planned for, or thrown out entirely. I resolved then and there to become less of a worrier and more of a planner. Over the years, I have faced things that I wouldn't have thought I could possibly deal with, but by making a plan instead of worrying I have always been able to find ways to shift to a new situation.

Some people seem to think that worry is like a cloak that will protect them, as if worrying about it enough will stop it from happening. But how much energy is spent during the worrying process? Especially if whatever you're worrying about never actually happens! And if the feared trouble does happen, you need all of your energy and faculties to deal with it most effectively, don't you?

Try to catch yourself whenever you find yourself giving energy over to worry states. Ask yourself what you are really worrying about and whether it's something you could use the S.H.I.F.T. Model™ to deal with. If you have specific obstacles you are facing and you are concerned about how to address them, use the process again to highlight them, organize them, and then methodically create a plan to remove them. Worrying, if you can turn it into a trigger that helps you plan, can be productive.

A common dynamic I see with some of the professional people I work with occurs when there are changes looming in their work environment and they are feeling the fear of what might happen to them. Fear of the unknown overwhelms them and they find themselves fixating on the worst possibility of what could go wrong. When this dynamic takes shape, the process of worrying hampers their ability to be a top performer, because the worry begins to affect their day-to-day abilities. Someone who may have been competent and confident is now slinking by their manager's door or fearfully watching the faces of senior managers in a meeting. Their fear takes on a life of its own, and the person could be labeled as someone who isn't confident enough for the next phase of the business, or even put on a list to be let go! Ultimately the worry has turned into a self-fulfilling prophecy.

As a result of these observations, I've come to understand that there aren't a lot of good reasons to worry, and that it zaps our emotional and physical strength when we let it consume us. Finding ways to focus your attention on more positive steps to take will ultimately benefit you much more than worrying will, no matter what you are facing.

To the degree that you can keep away from people who are gloom and doom, or away from reading undesirable things or watching TV programs with dire predictions, you will find you may be less worried in general. I'm not suggesting denial is a good state to be in, but if you are a person prone to worry, exposing yourself to those things that create more pointless fear and concern may be counterproductive.

It's important to be self-interested and learn to ask, "Is this good for me?" Start making choices that allow you to keep your energy and put it toward productive ends. In any job you want to be the best that you can be at all times; you never know who is watching. Managing your stress, learning to be more effective in spite of difficult conditions, can allow you to rise to the top of the list in terms of people the company can count on during difficulty.

"The way to get started is to quit talking and begin doing."
— Walt Disney

CHAPTER 10

Getting There From Here

Now that your team has completed all of the steps in the process, review what you've done in each section and capture it in one place. Use the worksheets in this chapter as a guide to compiling your plan for success.

1. Specify your desired outcome. Paint a clear and understandable picture of what you most desire and what success will look like when you get there. Remember to consider why this outcome is important for you to reach at this particular point in time. Evolve the desired outcome as much as you can, while keeping it realistic and measurable in some way so that you'll know that you have achieved it when you get there. Remember that you need your quantitative targets, but you need the qualitative ones, too. Take some time to envision what success looks like to your team or your firm. Be sure you don't stop with one discrete area; think about cause and effect. Be as clear and complete as you can possibly be.

2. Highlight your obstacles and categorize them. What prevents your team from doing what they want to do to be successful, this minute? What stands in the way? Productively brainstorm the obstacles from the past and the things you know that might stand in your way as you make your shift toward your desired outcome. Allow team members to voice their challenges and capture them. First list them and then categorize them: those you can control, those you can't control but can influence, and those you can't control. Be sure to capture themes as you organize the list.

3. Identify your internal and external human factors. First think about the internal aspect — what concerns or resistance do team members have about the change? And conversely, what strengths exist that will benefit you? Next look at the external stakeholders — who will care about the decisions you make, and what stake do they have in them? Remember to place the stakeholders on the scale of low to high interest and low to high power. Be sure to identify what their stake is and how it might impact your desire for change.

4. Find your alternatives. Review what your team has uncovered and captured in the first three steps of the process as you decide which options work for your situation. Brainstorm the possible ways to reach the desired outcome. What criteria do you have, and what is the priority order you want to apply to them? As you consider your criteria and review your list of possible alternatives, which one emerges as the best probability for making your shift?

5. Take disciplined action. What is your plan? What are the specific things you need to do that will help you get there from here in a step-by-step fashion? Who will complete each step? By when?

What will you do when you encounter an obstacle along the way? What budgetary issues do you need to plan for? How will you communicate progress to the rest of the team as the process of change unfolds?

In Summary

1. Specify your desired outcome.
2. Highlight your obstacles and categorize them.
3. Identify your internal and external human factors.
4. Find your alternatives.
5. Take disciplined action.

"Change starts when someone sees the next step."
— William Drayton

CHAPTER 11

Conclusion

Most companies have something they'd like to change within their system. The challenge is in figuring out what changes will actually take hold and have the impact the organization is counting on. Most teams and managers just identify a desire and then start to move confidently in the direction of that desire with their plan for success. Sometimes it works, but most of the time it doesn't. Chances are if you're reading this book, it's because you have had good intentions and have probably worked hard on change, but your plans haven't turned out as you have wanted. Without having a framework, a way of looking at your current situation and understanding where you want to go, you can spend a great deal of time and energy pushing against a mountain of seemingly insurmountable problems.

Assuming your goal in reading this book is to make a change for the better in your organization, you've just learned a process and some helpful tips for making your personal shift happen. Of course we can try to reach new ideas by trial and error—and eventually we may land on something that is workable for us, but using the S.H.I.F.T. Model™ can save a lot of time and effort.

Applying some of the ideas you picked up from Part II will also help you to get where you want to be faster and more efficiently than you might otherwise be able to manage. Part II should also get you thinking about ways in which you can improve yourself and your organization in the long term, offering new perspectives on how to self-manage and manage your teams more effectively.

The S.H.I.F.T. Model™ was designed to allow you to put your assumptions aside and figure out where you are and what you need to do to get your organization where you want it to be, helping you take methodical steps to put a plan in place that will work for you.

The S.H.I.F.T. Model™ is a great way to bring teams together, get employees focused on the same objectives, and move a static organization forward when it most needs it. The hardest part is often creating that disciplined plan that everyone can agree upon and take individual tasks, so be sure to capture all of the steps in detail before you begin. And as we know in life, oftentimes the most difficult part of any journey is taking the first step.

Let your team or organization take that first step today.

Business
Effectiveness Tools

BUSINESS PLAN OUTLINE

1. **Executive Summary**
   a. What is the purpose of the business plan?
   b. What is the reasoning for the proposed change or development outlined in the plan?
2. **Mission Statement and Objectives**
   a. What are your company's values?
   b. What are the objectives of the company?
   c. What are the primary goals, and who is primarily responsible for achieving them?
3. **Market Segment Analysis**
   a. Who are your customers?
   b. What markets do you intend to target with your business?
4. **Product/Service Information**
   a. What are the key benefits of the product or service you're offering?
   b. Why are these products or services different from everything else on the market?
   c. What is the need for these products or services?
   d. How was this need determined?
5. **Marketing Strategies**
   a. Who will the business advertise to?
   b. How will it advertise to its audiences?
   c. What are the marketing objectives?
   d. How will marketing success be recorded and assessed?
6. **Sales Strategies**
   a. Who will be responsible for sales?
   b. How will prospects be converted to sales?
   c. How will sales be recorded and increased if necessary?
7. **Personnel Information**
   a. Company structure?
   b. Key job descriptions?
   c. Personnel with positions of authority?
   d. Responsibilities and relevant skill sets assigned by person or by department?

INTERNAL BRANDING TIPS

1. What is the mission of your organization?
2. What are the key values of your organization?
3. Who is responsible for maintaining those values and achieving the mission?
4. How will responsibility be assigned?
5. How will progress toward the achievement of missions and the maintenance of values be monitored?
6. How will you communicate the mission and values?
7. How will you establish whether you are on track or off track?
8. What kind of culture do you want your internal brand to bring about?

PRESENTATION POINTERS

1. **Identify the why of the presentation.** Why now? Why this audience? Why are you presenting this information at this time? Outline what you hope to accomplish before you even begin.

2. **Identify the who.** What do you know about this audience? What matters to them? Why is this person or these people listening to you?

3. **Chunk the information.** What are your themes? How can you organize them into a handful of topics? What is the information under each topic?

4. **Make it matter — provide context.** How can you bring your information around to address the needs of this audience at this time? Why does this matter to them?

5. **Match behavioral style.** What is the communication style of your audience? How can you shift your approach to make the person or audience feel most comfortable? How can you transition during a presentation to a larger audience so that you insert different tones, styles, and communication approaches?

6. **Bring closure.** What do you want to have happen next? What is the outcome of your presentation? What do you want someone to do?

STRESS MANAGEMENT GUIDE

1. **Causes of Stress**
   a. What causes stress within your organization? List the things that you and members of your organization have found stressful over the past few weeks:
   b. What are the causes of chronic stress within your organization? List the biggest causes of stress for your organization over the past year or more:
   c. What stress factors are affecting your organization the most today?

2. **Stress Symptoms**
   a. How do you know when your organization as a whole is going through a stressful period?
   b. What are your early warning signs of stress? What are the first things you notice when your organization experiences stress?
   c. What are the chronic symptoms of long-term stress? Are there any symptoms your organization experiences often?

3. **Coping Skills and Habits**
   a. How do you handle stress brought on by work? List your usual coping habits.
   b. How does your organization handle stress? List common coping habits used.
   c. How effective are the coping behaviors you have used in the past? Do they reduce or eliminate the stress?
   d. Are there any coping techniques you or your organization used in the past but are no longer using?

4. **Changing Situations**
   a. Choose one of your stress causes. How can this situation be changed or improved? For example:
      • Relationship stress — assertive communication training, setting boundaries, resolving conflict
      • Overcommitment — setting boundaries, saying no, eliminating some things from your schedule
      • Grief and loss, personal/family issues — seeking support, journaling, finding enjoyable activities to fill your day

b. Describe your stressful situation.

c. How can this situation be changed or improved?

5. **Developing Effective Coping Strategies**

Not all stressful situations are within your control, and not every situation can be changed. Your organization needs to have strategies to be able to cope with stress in a healthy way. Healthy coping strategies include:

- relaxation techniques
- deep breathing exercises
- exercise
- yoga

a. List three coping strategies that have worked for you or your organization in the past that you would like to try and use regularly within your organization.

b. List three new coping strategies you would like to try within your organization.

c. When will you use these coping techniques within your organization?

d. What are your goals in applying these coping mechanisms regarding your stress levels?

e. What changes do you hope to see as a result of using these coping strategies?

About the Author

Beverly D. Flaxington is an accomplished business consultant, corporate coach, trainer, facilitator, behavioral expert, hypnotherapist, college professor, and business development expert.

Bev co-founded The Collaborative, a sales and marketing consultancy, and is currently principal of the firm. Beverly is the creator of "The Sales Effectiveness Model" used by many client firms to help diagnose areas of weakness and implement more effective selling practices. She trademarked the S.H.I.F.T. Model™ for goal setting, and The Five Secrets to Successful Selling™ program.

Beverly is a Certified Professional Behavioral Analyst (CPBA) and Certified Professional Values Analyst (CPVA). She uses the DISC and PIAV tools frequently in her work with individuals and organizations. Beverly's book, *Understanding Other People: The Five Secrets to Human Behavior*, won a gold award from Readers Favorite for best new book on relationships. She authored *The 7 Steps to Effective Business Building for Financial Advisors*. She is also the co-author of *Wealthbuilding: A Consumer's Guide to Making Profitable — and Comfortable — Investment Decisions*, published by Dearborn Financial Publishing.

Bev is a frequent contributor in the media and has been featured on:

Lifetime Television's Balancing Act, with Jordan Rich on WBZ Radio, on Doc Michelle of LA Talk Radio with Dr. Jackie Black of BlogTalk Radio, and on WVOL 1470 AM, Nashville, TN: "Differences" with Deniece Barnes; WEUS 810 AM, Orlando, FL: "The Shannon Burke Show"; WFSX 92.5 FM Fox News Radio, Ft. Meyers-Naples, FL: with Doug Kellett; KKZZ 1400 AM, Ventura, CA: with Billy Frank aka Billy The Brain; WBT 1110 AM/99.3 FM, Charlotte, NC: "Morning News Weekend" with Don Russell; CRN (Cable Radio Network): "The Talk Back Show with Chuck Wilder"; KAHI 950 AM, Auburn/Sacramento, CA: KAHI Noon News with Dave Rosenthal; KBIQ Q102.7 FM, Colorado Springs, CO: with Megan Goodyear; WCUB 980 AM/WLTU 92.1 FM, Multiple Cities, WI: "The Breakfast Club" with Dean & Bryan; KAHI 950 AM, Auburn/Sacramento, CA: "PoppOff" with Mary Jane Popp; WINA 1070 AM, Charlottesville, VA: "The Schilling Show" with Rob Schilling; KPCW 91.9 FM, Park City, UT: with Larry Warren; CRN (Cable Radio Network): The Gary Baumgarten Report; WONC 89.1 FM, Naperville, IL: "Newsmakers"; CVBT (Central Valley Business Times): with Doug Caldwell; WCHE 1520 AM, West Chester, PA: "The WCHE Wake Up Call" with Matt Lombardo; KRLD, Dallas, TX: with Bonnie Petrie and Dave Rancken.

Articles about her and her views have appeared in:

The Boston Globe, Readers Digest, Selling Power Magazine, and SheKnows.com with Michele Borboa; Opposing Views.com with Mike McNulty; FoxNews.com; ABCNews.com

Ready for more?

Visit Bev at **www.understandingotherpeople.com** and at **www.the-collaborative.com** to learn more about workshops, products, and facilitation services or to hire Bev to speak at your company.

To learn more about communicating effectively in both work and personal settings, get a copy of Bev's book, *Understanding Other People: The Five Secrets to Human Behavior.*

Made in the USA
Charleston, SC
29 December 2011